Great Cruise Ships and Ocean Liners from 1954 to 1986

• A PHOTOGRAPHIC SURVEY •

by William H. Miller, Jr.

Dover Publications, Inc., New York

TO ARNOLD KLUDAS, WHO,

IN HIS MANY BOOKS,

HAS GIVEN US A

TREMENDOUS RESOURCE.

Great Cruise Ships and Ocean Liners from 1954 to 1986: A Photographic Survey is a new work, first published by Dover Publications, Inc., in 1988.

Manufactured in the United States of America
Dover Publications, Inc.,
31 East 2nd Street,
Mineola, N.Y. 11501

Library of Congress Cataloging-in-Publication Data

Miller, William H.
Great cruise ships and ocean liners from 1954 to 1986.

Bibliography: p.
Includes index.
1. Cruise ships. 2. Ocean liners. 3. Cruise ships—
Pictorial works. 4. Ocean liners—Pictorial works.
I. Title.
VM381.M447 1987   387.2′432   87-22353
ISBN 0-486-25540-9 (pbk.)

Acknowledgments

MANY HANDS have assisted in assembling this pictorial record. The author wishes to make special mention of three eminent passenger-ship historians and authors: Frank O. Braynard, John Maxtone-Graham and Hisashi Noma. Their inspiration has been especially important. Each of these gentlemen, in his own way, has contributed to a special understanding of the great ships presented here. Furthermore, a group of skillful marine photographers has given unfailing help: J. K. Byass, Michael Cassar, Alex Duncan, Michael D. J. Lennon, B. Reeves, A. Scrimali and Roger Sherlock. A number of the world's great collectors of ocean-liner material have also been most supportive: Herbert G. Frank, Jr., Vincent Messina, Richard K. Morse and J. F. Rodriguez.

Other forms of assistance, pieces of information and kind cooperation came from Erwin Abele; Donald V. Reardon of the American President Lines; Ernest Arroyo; Cecil Spanton Ashdown; Robert H. LeMay of the Bethlehem Steel Company; Claire Bottino; James Ciani; the Companhia Portuguêsa de Transportes Marítimos, Lisbon; Neil Osborne and Susan Alpert of the Cunard Line; Francis J. Duffy; Terri Smythe of the Farrell Lines; Captain James L. Fleishell; the Hapag-Lloyd Shipyards; R. Izawa; Julie Ann Low; Charles Regal of the Matson Navigation Company; George McDermott; Y. Minami; Chris Montegriffo; William North; Thomas J. Olds of the Newport News Shipbuilding & Dry Dock Company; Fran Sevcik of Norwegian Caribbean Lines; Len Wilton and David Llewhellin of P & O Cruises, London; Thomas C. Young of the Port Authority of New York & New Jersey; J. J. Vernon and Jean Datin of the Port of Le Havre Authority; William Rau; Roger Scozzafava; Victor Scrivens; James M. Sesta; Peter Smith; Sheila Ballantyne, Glenda Thomas and Peter Ashton of the Southern Newspapers, Limited, Southampton; Clifford Morgan of the United States Lines; Everett Viez; James Dawson and the Virgin Islands Port Authority; Göran Damström of the Wärtsilä Shipyards; Howard E. Whitford; Barry Winiker; the World Ship Society Photo Library and V. H. Young.

Of course, and hardly least, my deepest appreciation to my family and to the expert staff at Dover Publications, especially James Spero.

Sources and Photographers

Ackroyd Photography, Inc.: 57 (top).
Air News Photos: 109 (bottom).
American Export Lines: 56.
American President Lines: 26, 27, 91 (top).
Cecil Spanton Ashdown Collection; 29, 60.
Stewart Bale: 8, 72 (top).
Bethlehem Steel Company: 82 (bottom).
Frank O. Braynard Collection: 14 (bottom), 15, 24, 33, 55 (top), 58 (bottom), 69 (bottom), 70 (bottom), 77 (top), 80 (bottom), 83.
J. K. Byass: 22 (top).
J. Allan Cash: 20 (bottom).
Michael Cassar: 48, 50, 51, 63 (bottom), 64 (top), 110 (bottom).
James Ciani: 85 (top).
Robert E. Coates: 28 (bottom).
Companhia Portuguêsa de Transportes Marítimos: 42, 43.
Cunard Line: 5 (top, right), 6 (top), 16, 18, 87 (bottom), 88, 89 (top), 115 (bottom).
Delta Line: 109 (bottom).
Alex Duncan: 32 (bottom), 49 (middle; bottom), 55 (middle), 63 (middle), 104 (bottom), 107.
Elsam, Mann & Cooper, Ltd.: 74 (top).
Engler: 37.
Epirotiki Lines: 103 (middle).
Europe-Canada Line: 37.
Everton: 77 (bottom), 84, 100 (left).
Farrell Lines: 25.
Flying Camera, Inc.: 2/3, 104 (top, right).
Herbert G. Frank, Jr., Collection: 19 (bottom), 36, 38 (bottom), 39, 46/47, 57, 76 (top), 91 (bottom).
French Line: 41 (top), 66/67.
Grace Line: 34.
Hapag-Lloyd Shipyards: 93 (top; middle).
E. A. Hof: 36.
Holland-America Line: 113 (top).
George Holton: 114 (top).
Island Navigation Company: 87 (top).
Italian Line: 80 (top).
Italian Line Cruises International: 104 (top, right).
John Jochimsen, Ltd.: 88 (right).
Eric Johnson: 61 (top).
C. Kramer: 38 (bottom).
Landis Aerial Surveys: 86 (bottom).
B. C. W. Lap: 76 (top), 91 (bottom).
Michael D. J. Lennon: 38 (top), 52 (bottom), 93 (bottom).
Matson Navigation Company: 58 (top, left).
Terence J. McNally: 52 (top).
Vincent Messina Collection: 17 (bottom), 87 (bottom).
Miami-Metro Department of Publicity and Tourism: 103 (top).
Y. Minami: 110 (top).
Chris Montegriffo: 111.
Richard K. Morse Collection: 2, 3, 9 (top), 10, 18/19 (top), 40/41 (bottom).

Newport News Shipbuilding and Dry Dock Company: 100 (left).
Nixon: 15 (bottom).
Hisashi Noma Collection: 44 (bottom).
North German Lloyd: 17 (top), 22 (bottom).
Norwegian-America Line: 101 (top), 105.
Norwegian Caribbean Lines: 113 (bottom).
P & O Group: 20 (bottom), 21, 71, 72, 73.
David E. Pettit Collection: 8.
Polish Ocean Lines: 106 (top).
Port Authority of New York & New Jersey: 4 (left), 6 (bottom), 7 (top), 9 (bottom), 68, 78, 79 (bottom), 102.
Port of Le Havre Authority: 89 (bottom), 92.
Princess Cruises: 109 (top).
Queen Mary Hyatt Hotel: 86 (bottom).
William J. Rader: 56.
William Rau Collection: 32 (top).
B. Reeves: 90 (bottom).
J. F. Rodriguez Collection: 14 (top).
Roland Rose: 100 (right).
Morris Rosenfeld: 24, 25.
Royal Caribbean Cruise Lines: 96, 97, 116.
Royal Cruise Lines: 108.
Royal Viking Line: 106 (bottom).
Roger Scozzafava: 61 (bottom).
A. Scrimali: 62.
Victor Scrivens Collection: 70 (top).
James M. Sesta Collection: 54.
Roger Sherlock: 20 (top), 55 (bottom), 64 (bottom), 76 (bottom), 79 (top), 103 (bottom).
Shipping Corporation of India, Limited: 44 (top).
Peter Smith Collection: 69 (top).
Southern Newspapers, Limited: 31, 81, 82 (top), 90 (top), 94, 101 (bottom).
Scott Stuart: 85 (top).
Swedish American Line: 104 (top, left).
Thigpen: 28/29 (top).
Trans-Atlantic Passenger Steamship Conference: 5 (bottom), 7 (top).
J. Uklejewski: 106 (top).
Union-Castle Line: 74, 75.
United States Line: 4/5 (top, center), 11, 12, 13, 52 (top), 77 (bottom).
Henri Van Wandelen: 26 (top).
Everett Viez Collection: 100 (right).
Virgin Islands Port Authority: 114 (bottom).
Bob Wands: 114 (bottom).
Wärtsilä Shipyards: 98, 99, 112
Steffen Weirauch: 115 (top).
Howard E. Whitford: 86 (top).
World Ship Society Photo Library: 63 (top).
V. H. Young: 30 (top).
Zim Lines: 49 (top).

Contents

Foreword, by Hisashi Noma

viii

Preface

ix

The Fifties: Prosperity

1

Combination Passenger-Cargo Vessels

23

The Working Ships

35

Emerging Flags

45

Face-lifts and Rebuildings

53

The Last of the Great Parade

65

The Cruise Ships

95

Bibliography

117

Alphabetical List of Ships Illustrated

118

Foreword

AFTER 30 YEARS in the study of the history and economics of merchant shipping, I made the acquaintance of another energetic enthusiast, Bill Miller. Since the late 1970s, we have been enjoying a friendship across the Pacific, exchanging correspondence that embodies our mutual fascination with passenger ships. In this, his latest work, the author has accomplished the feat of depicting the transition of passenger shipping to its current status, portraying the dramatic changes of the ocean liner, from the woeful withdrawal of the great Atlantic liners and others to the creation of the contemporary cruise-ship era.

Nothing in the history of world transportation has ever been subjected to a more radical change than the role played by passenger ships between the 1950s and 1970s. The great *Liberté,* that symbol of French liberty; the grand Cunard Queens (including the first and the last of the Atlantic titans); the *Michelangelo* and *Raffaello,* white goddesses born in a land of superb artists—all these famous ocean liners received the fatal blow from the villain called the commercial jet aircraft. After failing to find a haven in the cruise trades, these ships were forced into the scrap yard—modern dinosaurs.

Although loyal fans bade farewell to each ship with a feeling of bereavement, they felt an expectant joy in anticipating their successors. Among my personal recollections is a statement made by a French consul in April 1959, on the occasion of the "demolition ceremony" of the *Furansu Maru,* the former *Ile de France,* which was ending her days in Osaka Bay. He stated: "The guests here may assume that we [the French people] are in sorrow at losing this great liner. However, it is not true. On the contrary, we regard the occasion as a pleasing and momentous event leading to the birth of our new child now being built. As you may know, our new *France* will be launched next May." The chapters in this book narrate how some mourned the old, such as the transatlantic fleet, but turned with expectation to the new cruising armadas that followed.

The earlier liners had been defeated by air travel, but new life was vested in some of the remaining passenger ships. After thorough face-lifting or rebuilding, they were sent on lucrative cruises to appealing tropic ports. Then, in rather quick succession, a new fleet of specifically built cruise ships appeared, highly specialized vessels with spacious lido and swimming-pool areas, more varied public accommodations, all first-class quarters and comfortable staterooms complete with private bathrooms. With the advent of these new cruise liners, deluxe shipboard life, accessible only to first-class passengers in the heyday of Atlantic service, has become available for the enjoyment of all passengers. In other words, the "millionaires' ship" *Caronia* of the fifties has virtually turned into "everyone's ship" today.

Passenger ships continue to play an important role in promoting the social and industrial development of mankind. Studying the history and the current status of passenger shipping, we can easily observe the important role played by the United States. In both transatlantic and transpacific liner trades, it attracted enormous numbers of immigrants, providing the means for many steamer firms to remain in business. At present, the number of American passengers taking cruises aboard ships of many nationalities is once again staggering.

This pageant of fine photographs gives passenger-ship enthusiasts a full coverage of the most attractive mode of transportation ever known.

HISASHI NOMA

Tokyo
1988

Preface

IN 1973, I had the good fortune to travel from New York to Le Havre on the legendary *France*. She was then just a little over ten and, much like fine wine, she had matured well. She was the reigning queen of the North Atlantic and probably of the world: the largest ship afloat, thoroughly luxurious and with that unrivaled chic possessed by a select few ships. Powerfully, yet with a particular grace and gentleness, she raced across the ocean—the last ship designed specifically as a transatlantic commuter. She was in every way the express liner. Her passengers had a sense of purpose in traveling to a specific destination. It was all part of the thrill, the electric experience.

However, the *France*—like so many before and around her—was doomed. Jet aircraft, an unbeatable rival, mercilessly killed off almost all the traditional passenger-ship routes. The great ocean liners—those grand old three- and four-stackers—the colonial ships, the mail boats, the combination types and even the troopships—became part of the past. Consequently, in the sixties and seventies entire fleets steamed off either to new employment (primarily as restyled and refitted cruise ships) or, more dramatically, to the scrap heap.

Fortunately, there are some healthy survivors, possibly lacking the personality and mystique of the earlier liners, but survivors at any rate. Present cruise ships, the last generation of major liners, are a fine group whose longevity is ensured by a growing tourist and leisure market. These ships are destinations within themselves—sleek, often white "floating hotels" with vast lido decks, tiled swimming pools, festive lounges and quiet rooms, ample staterooms and gourmet restaurants, all combined with a range of on-board amusements from wine tasting to aerobic dancing—visiting colorful and tropical ports much more for diversion than any sense of destination.

Despite all the recent changes, one aspect remains: Three mighty blasts on the whistle, the ship begins to move away from the dockside, a tug pushes at the bow and an experience is about to begin that, no matter how short, is still matchless.

WILLIAM H. MILLER

Note

The statistics given for some of the liners may not necessarily agree with those given in other works. Many liners underwent considerable and frequent changes during their careers, which often altered their tonnages, speeds and passenger capacities and configurations. Except where noted otherwise, the statistics quoted here are those applicable to the period in question.

The Fifties: Prosperity

THE FIFTIES was the last decade of great prosperity for most of the world's ocean liners and their port-to-port services. In 1958, 1.2 million people crossed the North Atlantic by ship—the greatest number in history. Other routes also flourished: Australia, Latin America, the African trades, transpacific and even the last remnants of the old colonial runs. The giant Cunard Queens, among the most outstanding examples, turned in a profit of more than $300,000 on each round-trip Atlantic voyage.

With such encouragement, each year a new flotilla of luxury ships appeared and seemed warranted. Sleeker and more modern than ever, they sailed from the shipyards: single-stackers, masts moved above the bridge, sharply raked bows. Britain's *Southern Cross* (1954) was the first major liner to have her funnel and engines aft. In the same year, P & O's 29,000-ton *Orsova* discarded the conventional mast completely. In 1959, the Dutch *Rotterdam* eliminated the conventional funnel and used instead twin side-by-side uptakes for her exhausts.

The liner ports of New York, Southampton, Le Havre, Lisbon, Naples and even far-off Sydney were busier than ever: On many occasions six and eight passenger ships might be berthed together. Aircraft were increasing, but few steamship lines took serious notice.

"LUXURY LINER ROW."

New York was the most important terminal port for the Atlantic liner trade. The great passenger ship piers along Manhattan's West Side, extending from West 44th to West 57th Streets, were familiarly known as "Luxury Liner Row." July 10, 1958, when the photograph was taken, was the busiest ocean-liner sailing day at New York since the end of the Second World War. Eight liners were moored together. The Italian Line's *Vulcania* is in the foreground; beyond is the *Constitution* of American Export Lines; the *America* and *United States* of the United States Lines; the *Olympia* of the Greek Line; the *Queen Elizabeth* and *Britannic* of Cunard; and the *Ocean Monarch* of Furness-Bermuda Line at the far end.

FIRST CLASS

"Luxury Liner Row" *(above, left)*. Locals, particularly motorists along the West Side Highway, became quite familiar with the great liners that berthed along Manhattan's western shore. In a scene dating from October 4, 1955, photographed from the roof of the McGraw-Hill Building on West 42nd Street, are (left to right): the *Flandre* of the French Line and three Cunarders: the *Mauretania, Queen Mary* and *Britannic*.

SAILING FROM NEW YORK.

The giant *Queen Mary (opposite, top right)*, with a capacity load of 1,995 passengers, slips from her Manhattan berth. The liners generally spent between 24 and 48 hours in New York. During that time, arriving passengers were cleared by customs and sent ashore. The public rooms and cabins were freshened and made ready for the next set of guests. Quantities of high-grade cargo were often handled as well. A return load would then be put aboard.

On the day of departure for Europe, passengers and visitors were allowed aboard about three hours prior to sailing time. However, they boarded in different groups, determined by class of accommodation. There were even separate entrances for first-class visitors, cabin-class visitors and tourist-class visitors. During the fifties, each visitor was charged 50 cents (which was donated to the seamen's fund of the ship's nationality).

At sailing time, the great liners were filled with activity: bon-voyage parties; deliveries of telegrams, fresh flowers and baskets of fruit; news interviews with celebrities; distribution of baggage (including those vast steamer trunks), making dining-room and deck-chair reservations (and even last-minute adjustments of state-room assignments in the purser's office). Then, 30 minutes before sailing, the whistles sounded, warning visitors to make their way ashore and passengers to go to the open decks for the final send-off.

As the *America* leaves its berth in the mid-fifties *(above, middle)*, passengers line the outside decks while waving; relatives and friends, some probably tearful, crowd the pier's outer end for that final exchange of farewells.

LEAVING PORT.

Cunard's *Mauretania (opposite, bottom)* undocks from "Luxury Liner Row" on April 7, 1959, and begins a voyage southward along the Hudson River to the Lower Bay and finally into the open Atlantic. In six days she will cross to Ireland and France, and in seven to England. In the background, from left to right, are Cunard's *Media, Queen Mary* and *Ivernia;* the French *Liberté;* the *United States;* and Italy's *Giulio Cesare.*

Leaving Port. Outbound liners often passed one another just off the Statue of Liberty (*right*). Here the *Hanseatic* of the Hamburg-Atlantic Line vies with Cunard's *Parthia*.

Five liners sailed from New York within 30 minutes of one another on the morning of July 12, 1956 (*opposite, bottom*). To the left is the *Flandre* of the French Line and in the center is the *Queen Elizabeth*. To the right is the *New York* of the Greek Line. Farther beyond, still along the Lower Hudson, are Holland-America's *Ryndam* and the *Giulio Cesare*.

THE CUNARD QUEENS.

During the fifties, Britain's Cunard Line had the mightiest fleet of liners on the North Atlantic—12 in 1957. Its ships carried a third of all passengers who crossed "the great pond," as the Atlantic was often called. Of course, the famed Queens—the *Mary* (*opposite, top*) and the *Elizabeth* (*above*)—with their weekly runs from New York or Southampton via Cherbourg, were the most illustrious and popular. The fleet mates (they were not sister ships) paid and then repaid their costs and were worthy of being the flagships of the mighty British merchant marine.

The Queens were probably the most socially prominent and newsworthy Atlantic liners. Traveling incognito, actress Greta Garbo disembarked from the *Queen Mary* at New York disguised as a stewardess. Charlie Chaplin began his self-imposed exile from America by sailing on the *Queen Elizabeth* for England. Queen

Elizabeth The Queen Mother sailed round-trip in the liners on a goodwill visit to the United States. Helena Rubinstein accidentally threw a used tissue box out of one of the *Queen Elizabeth*'s portholes—a box that contained a pair of her 20-carat diamond earrings. The young Jacqueline Bouvier (later Mrs. John F. Kennedy) sailed tourist class on the *Queen Elizabeth* for a summer tour of Europe. The list is endless: Churchill, Lord Mountbatten, the Eisenhowers, the Windsors, Elizabeth Taylor, Noel Coward, Laurel and Hardy, the King of Arabia, Aristotle Onassis and even a Texas oil baron who insisted on fried rattlesnake in the first-class grill.

On a summer morning, the *Queen Elizabeth* (*opposite, top*) is in mid-Hudson, about to sail on a five-day run to France and England. In the background, at the Manhattan piers, from left to right, are the *Italia* (Home Lines); *Kungsholm* (Swedish-American Line); *Queen of Bermuda* (Furness-Bermuda Line); *Georgic, Mauretania* and *Caronia* (Cunard); and the *Olympia* (Greek Line). [*Queen Elizabeth:* Built by John Brown & Company, Limited, Clydebank, Scotland, 1940. 83,673 gross tons; 1,031 feet long; 119 feet wide; 39-foot draft.

Steam turbines, quadruple screw. Service speed 28.5 knots. 2,283 passengers (823 first class, 662 cabin class, 798 tourist class).]

Among the first-class amenities on each Queen, passengers could dine in the special Veranda Grill for a slight additional fee. The grill offered a setting of luxurious isolation for duchesses and movie moguls, ambassadors and corporate tycoons. It was positioned at the aft end of the boat deck, its large windows offering an imposing panoramic view of the sea and the liner's wake.

However, the Queens were not without their operational problems, no matter how slight. Since the liners were not fully air-conditioned, summer voyages were often quite warm in below-deck quarters. Aboard the *Queen Mary* (*above, top*) it often took as long as 48 hours to cool down following a July or August departure from New York. [*Queen Mary:* Built by John Brown & Company, Limited, Clydebank, Scotland, 1936. 81,237 gross tons; 1,019 feet long; 119 feet wide; 39-foot draft. Steam turbines, quadruple screw. Service speed 28.5 knots. 1,995 passengers (711 first class, 707 cabin class, 577 tourist class).]

The *Queen Elizabeth.* Both Queens were glittering examples of "Transatlantic Deco." Indirect lighting, lacquered surfaces and highly polished floors accentuated the beauty of the first-class main foyer on the *Queen Elizabeth.*

THE FRENCH LINE (left).

The *Liberté* (here departing from "Luxury Liner Row" on July 9, 1958, with the *Mauretania* and *Queen Elizabeth* still at berth) was the French Line's champion ship during the fifties. Her running mate was the slightly smaller, yet equally celebrated, *Ile de France*. A third ship—the tourist-minded, 20,000-ton *Flandre*—assisted during the peak summer season. Together, the trio provided weekly sailings in each direction between Le Havre and New York, with stopovers at either Southampton or Plymouth.

Just as in the twenties and thirties, the French Line had a particularly grand flavor—all smartness and chic. Elegance seemed to be synonymous with its ships, in terms of both superb decoration and flawless service. Of course, the cuisine, just as in the past, made their passengers the best-fed on the Atlantic. In terms of acclaim and popularity, the *Liberté* fell just short of Cunard's Queens. Originally the *Europa* of the North German Lloyd line, the ship had been given to the French Line as a war reparation. [*Liberté*: Built by Blohm & Voss Shipyards, Hamburg, Germany, 1930. 51,839 gross tons; 936 feet long; 102 feet wide; 34-foot draft. Steam turbines, quadruple screw. Service speed 24 knots. 1,502 passengers (555 first class, 497 cabin class, 450 tourist class).]

After strenuous wartime service as a troopship, the *Ile de France* was renovated and redecorated. Some of her furnishings came from the *Normandie*, the French giant that had burned at her New York pier in February 1942.

In her refitting of 1948–49, the *Ile* had a late Art Deco flavor, sleeker and less pretentious than in her prewar days. The first-class library (*above*) reflected her new style.

The French Line. Another public space aboard the *Ile de France* (*above*) was the grand salon.

The first-class grand salon (*right*) on the *Flandre* was completely contemporary in style. Commissioned in 1952, she was the French Line's first postwar liner. [Built by Ateliers et Chantiers de France, Dunkirk, France, 1952. 20,469 gross tons; 600 feet long; 80 feet wide; 26-foot draft. Steam turbines, twin screw. Service speed 22 knots. 784 passengers (402 first class, 285 cabin class, 97 tourist class).]

UNITED STATES.

America's flagship, the *United States,* enjoyed enormous popularity during the fifties, particularly as she was the fastest liner in the world and holder of the coveted Blue Ribbon. Her record run, in July 1952, took three days, ten hours and 40 minutes between the Ambrose Lightship, New York, and Bishop Rock, England. She took the trophy from the *Queen Mary,* a distinction that had been held by the British liner since 1938. The *United States* was, in fact, the last liner to take the Ribbon. She maintained a five-day schedule between New York, Le Havre and Southampton (and occasionally six days to Bremerhaven). The ship's popularity was also prompted by her flag. Many Americans preferred to travel on a national liner and, being of

the superliner class, she was an obvious rival to the British Queens and France's *Liberté.*

In a morning view, three liners arrive on the Hudson. The *United States,* in the foreground, is about to dock at Pier 86, at the foot of West 46th Street. The *Queen Mary,* behind her, is heading for Pier 90, at West 50th Street. In the distance, Holland-America's *Ryndam* is being turned by tugboats into her Hoboken, New Jersey, slip. [*United States:* Built by the Newport News Shipbuilding and Dry Dock Company, Newport News, Virginia, 1952. 53,329 gross tons; 990 feet long; 101 feet wide; 28-foot draft. Steam turbines, quadruple screw. Service speed 30–33 knots. 1,928 passengers (871 first class, 508 cabin class and 549 tourist class).]

The *United States*. Passengers enjoy mild weather during a crossing on the *United States* (*above*). For the average passenger, getting there was half the fun. There were long, lazy afternoons of reading and napping, and tea at four. After dinner, there might be some "horse racing" in the lounge or a film in the ship's theater.

Weather conditions on the North Atlantic were notorious—rain, wind, fog, hurricanes, gales, freak waves, even snowstorms. Consequently, the Atlantic liner fleet was designed mostly for indoor entertainment. Except for July and August, weather conditions could hardly be guaranteed.

World-famous celebrities often sailed on the *United States* in first-class suites, attended by servants. The Duke and Duchess of Windsor (*opposite, top left*) were the most-publicized transatlantic passengers during the fifties, making annual pilgrimages to New York aboard the *United States,* to which they were loyal. Then, after several weeks ashore, they returned aboard the liner, occupying the same suites, with their pug dogs and upwards of 90 pieces of luggage in tow. Although the Windsors occupied a superior suite in first class, they were often seen dancing in the lounges, strolling on deck and even entertaining fellow passengers at private parties.

Another New York celebrity arrives in New York on the *United States.* Actress Greta Garbo (*opposite, top right*) is escorted ashore in 1953.

Small armies of New York City's press welcomed inbound liners during the fifties. Former Hollywood film queen Grace Kelly (*opposite, bottom*) arrives as a royal princess aboard the *United States.* Left of her is her husband, Prince Rainier of Monaco.

AMERICA (opposite, top).

The older and smaller *America,* also of the United States Lines, was the running mate of the *United States.* However, because of differences of size and speed, the liners were forced to keep separate schedules that often placed them together in the same port.

The *America* attracted her own loyal following. The interiors of the ship were considerably more luxurious than the more functional, metallic stylings of the *United States.* Furthermore, the *America* offered a more leisurely Atlantic crossing—six days to Cobh, Ireland, seven days to Le Havre and Southampton and eight days to Bremerhaven. Here the *America* is docked at the Columbus Pier at Bremerhaven with the stern section of the Greek-owned *Olympia* to the right. [*America:* Built by the Newport News Shipbuilding and Dry Dock Company, Newport News, Virginia, 1940. 33,961 gross tons; 723 feet long; 94 feet wide; 29-foot draft. Steam turbines, twin screw. Service speed 22.5 knots. 1,046 passengers (516 first class, 530 tourist class).]

GIULIO CESARE (left, top).

The Italian Line was able to offer a weekly sailing from New York during the fifties, either on the express route to Gibraltar, Naples, Genoa and Cannes, or on the longer trip to Messina, Palermo, Dubrovnik, Venice and Trieste. One of the company's great advantages was a strong national following. Furthermore, its four largest liners were among the most modern on the Atlantic, all smart postwar designs that compared strikingly with the likes of prewar Cunarders and French liners. The new ships—the *Andrea Doria, Cristoforo Colombo, Augustus* and *Giulio Cesare*—capitalized on their modernity. The older fleet mates, such as the *Saturnia, Vulcania, Conte Biancamano* and *Conte Grande,* emphasized old-world charms and interiors.

The first-class main lounge (*opposite, bottom*) was starkly modern for the fifties transatlantic trade. [Built by Cantieri Riuniti dell'Adriatico, Monfalcone, Italy, 1951. 27,078 gross tons; 681 feet long; 87 feet wide. Fiat diesels, twin screw. Service speed 21 knots. 1,180 passengers (178 first class, 288 cabin class, 714 tourist class).]

CONSTITUTION (left, bottom).

American Export Lines' *Independence* and *Constitution* were extremely popular on the "Sunlane Route" between New York, Algeciras (Spain), Naples, Genoa and Cannes. Well-kept and sleek, yet without an overwhelming or oppressive sense of luxury, the sister ships were the first large American liners built for the busy Mediterranean trade. They presented serious competition to the Italian Line, which had long dominated the route. Even Italian immigrants, similar to those at the turn of the century who felt that an American vessel would ease entry into the new homeland, often preferred the Yankee pair to national ships. [Built by the Bethlehem Steel Company, Quincy, Massachusetts, 1951. 30,293 gross tons; 683 feet long; 89 feet wide; 30-foot draft. Steam turbines, twin screw. Service speed 23 knots. 1,110 passengers (405 first class, 375 cabin class and 330 tourist class).]

MEDIA (above).

During her winter overhaul in January 1953, Cunard's combination liner *Media* was fitted with Denny-Brown fin stabilizers, the first on a transatlantic passenger ship. Such fins greatly reduced rolling at sea, consequently limiting the extent of seasickness on board. The test met with great success; stabilizers were soon fitted on the *Queen Mary, Queen Elizabeth* and all new liners. [Built by John Brown & Company, Limited, Clydebank, Scotland, 1947. 13,345 gross tons; 531 feet long; 70 feet wide; 30-foot draft. Steam turbines, twin screw. Service speed 18 knots. 250 first-class passengers.]

BERLIN (opposite, top).

At the war's end in 1945, the North German Lloyd had lost its entire passenger-ship fleet; only two 1,200-ton freighters survived. With the release of Allied restrictions, the company began to rebuild slowly. It was not until 1954 that Atlantic passenger services resumed. The Swedish-American liner *Gripsholm* was first chartered, then bought outright a year later. She became the *Berlin,* the first German passenger ship to sail out of Bremerhaven since 1939. [Built by Sir W. G. Armstrong Whitworth & Company, Limited, Newcastle-upon-Tyne, England, 1925. 18,600 gross tons; 590 feet long; 74 feet wide; 29-foot draft. Burmeister & Wain diesels, twin screw. Service speed 16.5 knots. 976 passengers (98 first class, 878 tourist class).]

EMPRESS OF BRITAIN (opposite, bottom).

Canadian Pacific's *Empress of Britain* entered the Liverpool-Montreal service in April 1956, the first new liner to be built for that famous firm since the *Empress of Britain* of 1931. The new ship, having been christened by Queen Elizabeth II, was, among other features, the first fully air-conditioned liner sailing under the Union Jack.

For most of the year, the new *Empress* and her fleet mates plied the northern waters of the Atlantic on their voyages to and from Canada, taking advantage of the 1,000-mile run along the St. Lawrence River when sailing to and from Montreal. During the winters, the Empresses either terminated their crossings at Saint John, New Brunswick, or went cruising to the Caribbean from New York. [Built by the Fairfield Shipbuilding & Engineering Company, Glasgow, Scotland, 1956. 25,516 gross tons; 640 feet long; 85 feet wide; 29-foot draft. Steam turbines, twin screw. Service speed 20 knots. 1,054 passengers (160 first class, 894 tourist class).]

Bremerhaven. Columbuskaje

THE SINKING OF THE *ANDREA DORIA*.

The balanced schedules of the "Atlantic Ferry" were momentarily disrupted in 1956. Disaster struck just off Nantucket on the foggy night of July 25, when the eastbound Swedish-American liner *Stockholm* and the inbound Italian flagship *Andrea Doria* crossed each other's path. Fatally struck below the bridge, the Italian liner sank in the early morning hours of the next day (*above*). In all, 52 lives and the pride of the Italian merchant marine were lost. [*Andrea Doria:* Built by the Ansaldo Shipyards, Genoa, Italy, 1953. 29,083 gross tons; 700 feet long; 90 feet wide; 30-foot draft. Steam turbines, twin screw. Service speed 23 knots. 1,241 passengers (218 first class, 320 cabin class, 703 tourist class).]

The *Stockholm* (*opposite*) lost her bow and limped back to New York, her reputation scarred. Fitted with a new bow at a Brooklyn shipyard, she returned to service in December 1956. There also followed a half-year of legal wrangling over the loss of lives. Damage suits totaled $40 million. Eventually, the case was settled out of court in unpublicized hearings conducted under the watchful eye of the London underwriters.

Although the tragedy made sensational headlines, it hardly put a dent in the booming transatlantic liner business. Profitable times continued. [*Stockholm:* Built by A. B. Götaverken Shipyards, Gothenburg, Sweden, 1948. 12,644 gross tons; 525 feet long; 69 feet wide; 24-foot draft. Götaverken diesels, twin screw. Service speed 19 knots. 608 passengers (24 first class, 584 tourist class).]

SOUTHERN CROSS (opposite, top).
Another British liner, Shaw Savill Line's *Southern Cross,* was something of a "wonder ship" when launched by Queen Elizabeth II in 1954. The vessel had a number of pioneering features: She was the first major liner to mount funnel and engines so far aft (creating important midships passenger spaces), the first passenger ship with no provision for cargo whatsoever and the first major modern liner for all-tourist-class service. Even the service for which she had been designed was somewhat unique—continuous 75-day around-the-world voyages from Southampton to Australia and New Zealand, outward via South Africa and homeward via Panama and the Caribbean. [Built by Harland & Wolff, Limited, Belfast, Northern Ireland, 1955. 20,204 gross tons; 604 feet long; 78 feet wide; 25-foot draft. Steam turbines, twin screw. Service speed 20 knots. 1,100 tourist-class passengers.]

HIMALAYA (opposite, bottom).
Early in 1958, the liner *Himalaya,* shown arriving at Hong Kong, opened a new transpacific passenger service for Britain's P & O–Orient Lines, sailing from Sydney and Auckland north to San Francisco and Vancouver. This was a considerable extension to the firm's normal operations from England to Australia and the Far East. A year later, the ship left Sydney to inaugurate a new company run from Yokohama and Kobe in Japan, across to the North American West Coast and then to London via Colombo (Sri Lanka) and Bombay. Consequently, P & O–Orient was now able to advertise liner services that practically spanned the globe—in fact the biggest passenger-ship network ever. [Built by Vickers-Armstrong Shipbuilders, Limited, Barrow-in-Furness, England, 1949. 27,955 gross tons; 709 feet long; 91 feet wide; 31-foot draft. Steam turbines, twin screw. Service speed 22 knots. 1,159 passengers (758 first class, 401 tourist class).]

ORSOVA (above).
The *Orsova* of Britain's Orient Line, the last ship in the firm's postwar rebuilding program of three major liners for service between England and Australia, was completed in May 1954, at a cost of nearly $15 million—at the time a considerable sum for a British-built passenger ship. Handsome and distinctly modern, she was the first major liner to dispense with the conventional mast entirely. Instead, necessary rigging was attached to the large single stack. She is seen here at Vancouver. [Built by Vickers-Armstrong Shipbuilders, Limited, Barrow-in-Furness, England, 1954. 28,790 gross tons; 723 feet long; 90 feet wide; 30-foot draft. Steam turbines, twin screw. Service speed 22 knots. 1,503 passengers (694 first class, 809 tourist class).]

ROTTERDAM (above).

The Dutch commissioned their largest liner ever, the Holland-America Line flagship *Rotterdam,* late in the summer of 1959. To highlight the occasion, Crown Princess Beatrix was aboard for the maiden crossing to New York. The *Rotterdam* was a handsomely decorated liner, a late example of a "ship of state," rich in national art, design and imported woods. She also had one very noticeable distinction—she was the first transatlantic liner to dispense with the conventional funnel. Instead, twin uptakes placed aft in a side-by-side position were used for the exhausts. Some purists mourned the loss of the customary smokestack; others thought the novelty was a practical design element. Britain's P & O Lines were among those impressed. Twin uptakes were used on the company's new flagship, the *Canberra,* commissioned in 1961. [Built by Rotterdam Dry Dock Company, Rotterdam, The Netherlands, 1959. 38,645 gross tons; 748 feet long; 94 feet wide; 29-foot draft. Steam turbines, twin screw. Service speed 20.5 knots. 1,456 passengers (401 first class, 1,055 tourist class).]

BREMEN (right).

West Germany's new flagship *Bremen,* reconstructed from the French troopship *Pasteur,* first crossed the North Atlantic to New York in July 1959. On her maiden arrival in Manhattan, she passed the outbound *Berlin,* her national running mate. Now the North German Lloyd had a two-ship passenger operation.

However, by the late fifties, the impact of the jet could no longer be ignored. Quick to recognize the competition, the Germans emphasized that their new *Bremen* was, in fact, more of a "sea-going hotel," with endless amenities for a relaxed crossing. Jet travel hardly had the same creature comforts. But, in winter, Atlantic traffic grew more and more desolate. Fortunately, the design of the *Bremen* included provisions for lucrative, winter cruising from New York to the Caribbean. [Built by Chantiers de l'Atlantique, St. Nazaire, France, 1939. 32,336 gross tons; 697 feet long; 88 feet wide; 30-foot draft. Steam turbines, quadruple screw. Service speed 23 knots. 1,122 passengers (216 first class, 906 tourist class).]

Combination Passenger-Cargo Vessels

OFTEN KNOWN as the "combo," the combination passenger-cargo liner was a particularly popular outgrowth of the Second World War and the decade or so that followed. This type of vessel was by no means new, however. Such ships, with a balance between passengers and freight, had proven themselves in earlier periods. The postwar period saw the largest number ever, for they were needed to revitalize worldwide trade routes in their practical dual role.

These ships were extremely profitable. Passengers, usually carried in high-standard accommodations, were one source of substantial revenues. The ships often traded to ports avoided by the larger liners and also offered extensive round-trip, cruiselike sailings. The American-flag combination ships, in particular, were quite popular in this latter role, especially since they were fitted with such extra features as outdoor pools, full air-conditioning, substantial deck space and excellent first-class cabins with private bathroom facilities. The second source of income was derived from the cargo spaces, frequently in excess of 10,000 tons per ship. The ships' speeds, often about 17 knots, made them the rivals of, or slightly superior to, the freighters of the time.

Several steamer firms, notably the British, French and Dutch, built these ships well into the fifties because of their success and popularity. Unfortunately, they have now all but disappeared. First, new freighters with higher speeds snatched their cargoes. Then they were hard hit by the general slump in passenger shipping caused by the jet. In their final days, many worked the tramp trades and were often downgraded to 12-passenger freighter rank. For others, the end came with the technological transition to container-cargo shipping, with its mammoth, high-speed vessels. At the time of writing, only a mere handful of combination liners survive.

AFRICAN ENTERPRISE.

The American-flag Farrell Lines ran its twin sisters *African Endeavor* and *African Enterprise* (*opposite*) on the long-haul run from New York to South and East Africa. The full voyage, including lengthy stays at such ports as Capetown and Durban, averaged 65 days and cost $950 during the fifties. In this photograph, the *African Enterprise* arrives in port, about to be docked at Brooklyn's Erie Basin.

A double-bedded stateroom aboard the *African Enterprise* (*above*) is crisply decorated. [Built by Bethlehem Steel Company, Sparrows Point, Maryland, 1940. 7,997 gross tons; 492 feet long; 66 feet wide. Steam turbines, single screw. Service speed 16.5 knots. 98 first-class passengers.]

PRESIDENT POLK.

The American President Lines revived its around-the-world passenger service following the war with the "combo" sister ships *President Monroe* and *President Polk* (*above*). Complete voyages, made in 105 days, took the ships from New York to the Panama Canal, Mexico, California, Hawaii, the Orient, Southeast Asia, India, Pakistan, the Suez Canal, along the Mediterranean and then homeward across the Atlantic. A large outside double-berth stateroom (*opposite, top*) was simple, yet comfortable. The dining room (*opposite, bottom*) was intimate. [Built by the Newport News Shipbuilding and Dry Dock Company, Newport News, Virginia, 1940. 9,260 gross tons; 492 feet long; 70 feet wide; 27-foot draft. Steam turbines, single screw. Service speed 16.5 knots. 96 first-class passengers.]

ALCOA CAVALIER.

Sailing for the Alcoa Steamship Company (a division of the Aluminum Company of America), the *Alcoa Cavalier* (*above*) and her two twin sisters, the *Alcoa Clipper* and *Alcoa Corsair,* were redesigned for passenger-cargo service from standardized Victory-class freighter hulls. High-quality passenger accommodations were fitted, which included cabins (all with private bathroom facilities), handsome public rooms and outdoor deck spaces with a permanent swimming pool, particularly useful because the three ships spent much of their sailing time in the tropical ports of the Caribbean. The ships offered 18-day round-trip cruises out of New Orleans.

Of course, cargo was important in the Alcoa operation. Here the *Alcoa Cavalier* arrives at Mobile with a cargo of bauxite from Trinidad.

All of the passenger staterooms on the three Alcoa sister ships, such as this (*opposite*), were convertible from nighttime sleeping quarters to daytime living rooms. Most of the lower beds served as a sofa during the day. There was an extensive use of aluminum in the accommodations aboard the Alcoa ships. Missing was the traditional shipboard woodwork and veneers. [Built by Oregon Shipbuilding Corporation, Portland, Oregon, 1947. 8,481 gross tons; 455 feet long; 62 feet wide; 28-foot draft. Steam turbines, single screw. Service speed 16.5 knots. 95 first-class passengers.]

GOTHIC *(opposite, top; above).*

Britain's Shaw Savill Line operated four sister ships—the *Athenic, Ceramic, Corinthic* and *Gothic*—on the run from London to New Zealand via the Caribbean, Panama Canal and South Pacific. The ships were particularly fitted with refrigerated compartments for the homeward loads of lamb and mutton, and with general cargo provisions for large amounts of wool.

In 1953, the *Gothic,* repainted white, was chartered by the British government to serve temporarily as a royal yacht for Queen Elizabeth II's coronation tour of the Commonwealth. The Queen, Prince Philip and their official party occupied modified passenger cabins. Freshly refurbished for the royal voyage, a passenger lounge *(above)* was outfitted as the Queen's sitting room.

The Queen flew out to Bermuda in November 1953 and joined the *Gothic.* The ship then passed through the Panama Canal and began a tour of the South Pacific. After long and highly publicized stays in both New Zealand and Australia, the ship sailed westward to Sri Lanka, East Africa and Suez, ending its voyage at Malta the following May. There the Queen was presented with a delayed coronation present from the Royal Navy—the 400-foot-long yacht *Britannia,* intended for future overseas tours. [Built by Swan, Hunter & Wigham Richardson, Limited, Newcastle, England, 1948. 15,902 gross tons; 561 feet long; 72 feet wide. Steam turbines, twin screw. Service speed 17 knots. 85 first-class passengers.]

EXETER *(opposite, bottom).*

The American Export Lines operated the very popular "Four Aces"—the *Excalibur, Excambion, Exeter* and *Exochorda.* Among the best-designed combination ships refitted in the United States following the Second World War, they included outdoor pools, sizable open-air deck spaces, finely furnished lounges and large staterooms. As a team, they provided seven-week round-trip cruises out of New York to Spain, southern France, Italy, Egypt, Lebanon, Turkey and Greece. [Built by Bethlehem Steel Company, Sparrows Point, Maryland, 1944. 9,644 gross tons; 473 feet long; 66 feet wide; 27-foot draft. Steam turbines, single screw. Service speed 17 knots. 125 first-class passengers.]

BRASIL STAR (*opposite, bottom*).

The *Brasil Star* was one of four combination sister ships built in the late forties for London's Blue Star Line. Each had space for over 50 first-class passengers in addition to six holds for cargo. Outward, they carried general cargo, such as automobiles and machinery, to Rio de Janeiro, Santos, Montevideo and Buenos Aires. Homebound, their freezer compartments were filled with Argentine beef destined for the meat markets of Britain. Blue Star, as part of the Vestey Group, was a member of a corporate giant that also included ownership of the meat markets, the freezer warehouses and even the cattle ranches in Argentina. [Built by Cammell Laird & Company Limited, Birkenhead, England, 1947. 10,716 gross tons; 503 feet long; 68 feet wide; 31-foot draft. Steam turbines, single screw. Service speed 16 knots. 51 first-class passengers.]

    The smoking room (*opposite, top*) aboard the *Brasil Star*'s sister ship, the *Uruguay Star,* reflected postwar British shipboard decoration.

SANTA MONICA (*above*).

The American-flag Grace Line commissioned nine 52-passenger combination sister ships of the *Santa Monica* class in 1946. Three of them, the *Santa Clara, Santa Monica* and *Santa Sofia,* sailed on three-week Caribbean voyages. The other six, the *Santa Barbara, Santa Cecilia, Santa Isabel, Santa Luisa, Santa Maria* and *Santa Margarita,* traded on six-week runs to the west coast of South America. Although each ship carried a diverse range of cargo, from coffee and bananas to nitrates and frozen fish, they also appealed to many tourists. Part of the attraction lay in the unusual, romantic-sounding ports of call, such as Cartagena, Buenaventura, Callao, Valparaiso and Antofagasta. Among their passenger facilities was the large white square on the mainmast, used as a screen in the tropics for nighttime open-air motion pictures. [Built by the North Carolina Shipbuilding Corporation, Wilmington, North Carolina, 1946. 8,357 gross tons; 459 feet long; 63 feet wide; 27-foot draft. Steam turbines, single screw. Service speed 16 knots. 52 first-class passengers.]

Combination Passenger-Cargo Vessels **33**

SANTA MARIANA.

The *Santa Mariana* and her three sisters, the *Santa Maria, Santa Magdalena* and *Santa Mercedes,* were designed for the Grace Line's New York–west coast of South America operation. They were built in advance of the great growth of the container trade, when most South American ports were still unequipped for this modern method of cargo shipping. Consequently, the four ships carried their own container cranes on deck. Below deck, there was specific provision for bananas. [Built by Bethlehem Steel Company, Sparrows Point, Maryland, 1963. 14,442 gross tons; 547 feet long; 79 feet wide. Steam turbines, single screw. Service speed 20 knots. 119 first-class passengers.]

The Working Ships

WORKING SHIPS were, and to some extent remain, a breed of specialists. As passenger vessels, they often lacked the glamour and luster of the larger liners. Their accommodations were sometimes quite austere. Speeds were slower. Their purpose was to transport low-fare or specialty passengers—budget tourists, immigrants, repatriates, refugees, religious pilgrims, students, workers and even troops.

Some of these ships operated well beyond their usual span. Smaller and well-worn hulks often went out on the North Atlantic, South America or Australia trades. Some had been overnight coastal steamers reworked for month-long voyages to Buenos Aires or Sydney, most with immigrants, the outward voyage often paying for the ship's expenses and earning rich profits. Homebound, they frequently went empty. Their on-board facilities were usually cramped and Spartan, and the original capacities were generally more than tripled.

Other working ships were newer and more carefully built. They had distinct purposes: a balance of cargo and passengers, who were often divided into three, four or as many as five separate classes. Some vessels, fresh out of the shipyards, had been purposely designed for single-class immigrant and low-fare tourist trades. This group tended to be somewhat faster and more spacious.

With the advent of inexpensive charter jet flights, many of these ships have now drifted into oblivion. The era of long, crowded immigrant sailings to Australia, for example, is now past. However, in their better days, these less-famous, often less-remembered, ships succeeded by transporting large numbers and earning great sums.

GROOTE BEER (opposite, top).

Many American-built wartime freighters were out of work and had become surplus by the late forties. Among these, three Victory-class freighters passed into Dutch hands. At first, they were used as troopships. Then, in 1951, the original freight spaces were converted for 900 one-class passengers, most of them either immigrants or students. The large dormitories fitted throughout the three sister ships (the *Groote Beer, Waterman* and *Zuiderkruis*) actually outnumbered the regular cabins. The trio, owned by the Dutch government but managed by such private passenger-ship companies as the Holland-America Line, sailed from Rotterdam or Amsterdam to ports around the world—New York, Quebec, Australia, the Far East, South Africa and the Caribbean. [Built by the Permanente Shipyard, Richmond, California, 1945. 9,190 gross tons; 455 feet long; 62 feet wide; 28-foot draft. Steam turbines, single screw. Service speed 17 knots. 900 one-class passengers.]

VOLENDAM (opposite, bottom).

Holland-America's *Volendam* never returned to its prewar status as a first-rate passenger liner, but was used instead for single-class "austerity service." In the late forties and early fifties, she divided her time between sailings from Rotterdam to New York or Quebec City with students and immigrants, and during the winters, on longer runs with immigrants to Australia. She is shown at Rotterdam loading "new settlers" bound for Sydney. [Built by Harland & Wolff, Limited, Govan, Scotland, 1922. 15,434 gross tons; 579 feet long; 67 feet wide. Steam turbines, twin screw. Service speed 15 knots. 1,693 tourist-class passengers.]

SEVEN SEAS (above).

A former freighter rebuilt as an auxiliary aircraft carrier during the war, the *Seven Seas* was refitted as a passenger ship in the late forties and later sailed for West Germany's Europe-Canada Line. A subsidiary of the Holland-America Line, the ship worked the "low-fare" trades on the North Atlantic—from Bremerhaven, Rotterdam, Le Havre and Southampton to either Montreal or Halifax and New York. In later years, during the winter off-season, she sailed as a floating university on world cruises with students studying on board. She finished her career in the less glamorous role of a workers' accommodation ship in Rotterdam harbor. [Built by Sun Shipbuilding & Dry Dock Company, Chester, Pennsylvania, 1940. 12,575 gross tons; 492 feet long; 69 feet wide; 22-foot draft. Sulzer diesel, single screw. Service speed 16.5 knots. 1,007 passengers (20 first class, 987 tourist class).]

The Working Ships **37**

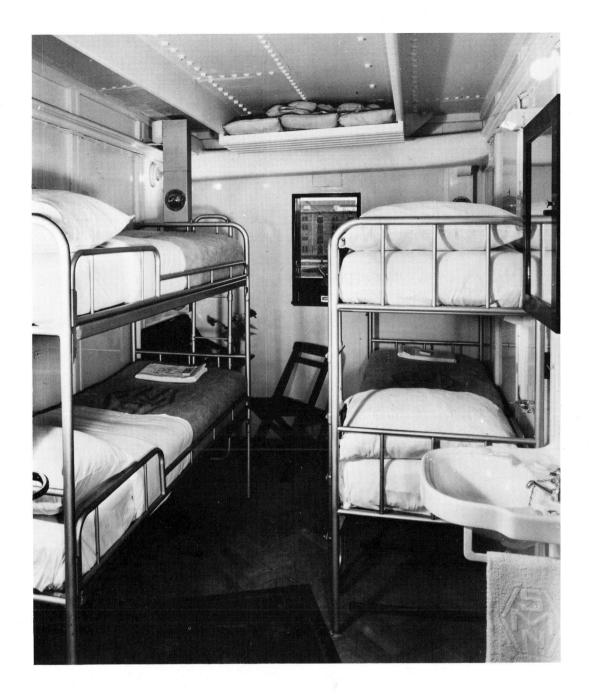

CABO SAN VICENTE *(opposite, top).*

Spain's Ybarra Line had long connections with the immigrant trade between Spain, other Mediterranean ports and the east coast of South America. In the late fifties, it commissioned its largest passenger ships yet, the sister ships *Cabo San Roque* and *Cabo San Vicente*. Their sailing patterns took them from Genoa, Barcelona, Palma de Mallorca, Cádiz, Lisbon and Tenerife across the South Atlantic to Rio de Janeiro, Santos, Montevideo and Buenos Aires. Along with very comfortable quarters in an intimate cabin class, their tourist sections, intended for westbound immigrants, were a substantial improvement over earlier ships. [Built by Sociedad Española de Construcción Naval, Bilbao, Spain, 1959. 14,569 gross tons; 556 feet long; 69 feet wide; 27-foot draft. Sulzer diesels, twin screw. Service speed 20 knots. 841 passengers (189 cabin class, 652 tourist class).]

SIBAJAK *(opposite, bottom).*

The Royal Rotterdam Lloyd liner *Sibajak* was originally designed for the colonial run from Amsterdam to the East Indies. After the war, she was converted to a one-class immigrant ship, usually trading to Australia. Outbound, she was often filled to capacity. Homeward, she sailed either empty or with returning passengers who were unhappy with their life "down under." [Built by De Schelde Shipyards, Flushing, Holland, 1928. 12,342 gross tons; 530 feet long; 62 feet wide. Sulzer diesels, twin screw. Service speed 17 knots. 1,000 one-class passengers.]

JOHAN VAN OLDENBARNEVELT *(above).*

On board another former Dutch colonial liner, the *Johan Van Oldenbarnevelt*, the postwar accommodations were restyled for immigrants and students. A typical four-berth cabin shows a certain lack of glamour. [Built by Netherlands Shipbuilding Co., Amsterdam, The Netherlands, 1930. 19,787 gross tons; 608 feet long; 74 feet wide; 27-foot draft. Sulzer diesels, twin screw. Service speed 17 knots. 1,414 one-class passengers.]

VILLE DE MARSEILLE *(opposite, top).*

The French Line's *Ville de Marseille,* a streamlined product of the company's postwar reconstruction program, worked the western Mediterranean to colonial Algeria. Crossing between Marseilles and the North African ports of Oran, Philippeville (now Skikda), Bône (now Annaba) and Algiers, she carried passengers ranging from rich traders and tourists to migrant workers and French troops. [Built by Forges et Chantiers de la Méditerranée, La Seyne, France, 1951. 9,576 gross tons; 466 feet long; 64 feet wide; 20-foot draft. Steam turbines, twin screw. Service speed 21 knots. 653 passengers (143 first class, 318 second class, 192 third class).]

IMPÉRIO *(right).*

Portugal's African colonies of Angola and Mozambique necessitated a fleet of liners that were divided between two firms, the Companhia Colonial and the Companhia Nacional. The Colonial's *Império* was a typical member of the fleets. She carried four classes of passengers (the lowest often being used for troops and police forces) and five holds of cargo. Service out of Lisbon took the *Império* and her fleet mates to three African coasts: first to São Tomé, Luanda, Lobito and Moçâmedes in Angola, then a stop at Capetown in South Africa, and then the eastern coast for calls at Lourenço Marques, Beira and Nacala in Mozambique. [Built by John Brown & Company, Limited, Clydebank, Scotland, 1948. 13,186 gross tons; 531 feet long; 68 feet wide; 28-foot draft. Steam turbines, twin screw. Service speed 18 knots. 590 passengers (114 first class, 156 tourist class, 320 third class.]

The *Império*. Designed for government officials, military leaders and prosperous merchants, the first-class section aboard the *Império* reflected a luxurious, very comfortable (but earlier) shipboard style. Shown here are the sitting room of the ship's best suite (*opposite, top*) and small first-class salon (*opposite, bottom*). The first-class smoking room lounge (*above*) was decorated in more contemporary style.

STATE OF MADRAS (above, top).

Bombay's Shipping Corporation of India, Limited, had its *State of Madras* assigned to local, short sea services. She shuttled sluggishly between Madras, Penang and Singapore. Some passengers went in so-called "saloon class" while the rest sailed in "steerage deck class." There were few provisions in the lower quarters—passengers even brought their own bedding. [Built by Swan, Hunter & Wigham Richardson, Limited, Wallsend, England, 1948. 8,580 gross tons; 456 feet long; 62 feet wide; 25-foot draft. Steam triple-expansion engines, twin screw. Service speed 13 knots. 650 passengers (150 saloon class, 500 steerage deck class).]

BRAZIL MARU (above, bottom).

A most unusual passenger run was the immigrant service between Japan and the east coast of South America. Tens of thousands of Japanese sought passage to Brazil and Argentina, either for resettlement or for special work projects. Although Japanese passenger lines did not build new tonnage for their traditional transpacific service to California after the war, they did build two specialized combination cargo-passenger-immigrant ships for the booming Latin American trade. One of these ships, the *Brazil Maru,* is shown leaving Kobe with a capacity load of immigrants bound for Rio de Janeiro, Santos and Buenos Aires. [Built by Mitsubishi Heavy Industries, Limited, Kobe, Japan, 1954. 10,100 gross tons; 512 feet long; 64 feet wide; 28-foot draft. Mitsubishi-type diesel, single screw. Service speed 16 knots. 982 passengers (12 cabin class, 68 tourist class, 902 third class).]

Emerging Flags

A FTER THE Second World War, a number of relatively rare flags of registry began to appear at the sterns of passenger ships. Generally, new shipowners were not aiming for enormous fleets or attempting to bask in national prestige. Their intentions were simpler: to dabble in some local trades, to meet specific passenger traffic requirements (such as those for immigrants or pilgrims) as a moderate investment in tourist cruising or, as in the cases of Panamanian and Liberian registry, to enjoy the convenience of lower taxes and to avoid the lofty costs of strict regulation under more traditional flags.

The most obvious exception in these growth patterns has been in the Soviet Union. Since the late forties, prompted by the pressing need for Western currencies, it has assembled the largest deep-sea passenger-ship fleet in the world. Soviet passenger ships are often charted to Western firms for relatively inexpensive cruise voyages.

In more recent times, some of these registries, such as Argentina, Israel and Portugal, have almost completely disappeared from passenger shipping because of politics, rising operational costs, aircraft competition and shifts in the passenger trade.

ABKHAZIA.

The Soviet passenger fleet has grown significantly since the end of the Second World War. At first, this was accomplished mostly by the seizure and salvage of sunken German passenger ships. In some instances, this was a tedious task, requiring years of work because of material shortages and sluggish operations at Soviet-controlled shipyards. Once completed, the ships were usually assigned to one of the three major Soviet passenger-ship runs: the local Black Sea service out of Odessa, the Baltic trade out of Leningrad or the more distant Siberian coastal trade out of Vladivostok. There were even occasional voyages to New York.

The *Abkhazia* was a postwar seizure, having been the German *Marienburg*. After a considerable refitting, she was based at Odessa for the coastal trade to Yalta, Sochi (where she is shown here) and Batumi. [Built by Stettiner Oderwerke Shipyard, Stettin, Germany, 1939. 6,807 gross tons; 431 feet long; 59 feet wide; 18-foot draft. Steam turbines, twin screw. Service speed 17 knots. Approximately 550 passengers.]

LEONID SOBINOV (above).

Although the Soviets began to build new passenger tonnage by the late fifties, they also periodically purchased secondhand liners. The *Leonid Sobinov,* the former Cunarder *Carmania,* was bought in 1973 and has since seen diverse service for her owners. At first, she was chartered to London's C.T.C. Lines for economy cruising from Britain as well as for immigrant voyages to Australia and New Zealand. Later, she ran in local Soviet service, mostly in the Black Sea. Then there were some crossings to Cuba with technicians and students and still later with Cuban soldiers to the Middle East and East Africa. Here she is shown at Valletta, Malta. [Built by John Brown & Company Limited, Clydebank, Scotland, 1954. 21,370 gross tons; 608 feet long; 80 feet wide; 28-foot draft. Steam turbines, twin screw. Service speed 19.5 knots. 881 one-class passengers.]

THEODOR HERZL (opposite, top).

Following its independence in 1948, Israel created its own passenger fleet, the Zim Lines. At first it consisted of old, smaller vessels, but through a West German reparations agreement, the company was given four new passenger ships in the mid-fifties. The first pair was the combination passenger-cargo liners *Israel* and *Zion,* both designed for the run between Haifa, the Mediterranean and New York. The second set of sister ships, the *Jerusalem* and *Theodor Herzl,* were created for local service between Haifa, Naples and Marseilles. Their primary purpose was to bring new settlers to the infant state of Israel. [Built by the Deutsche Werft Shipyard, Hamburg, West Germany, 1957. 9,914 gross tons; 488 feet long; 65 feet wide; 21-foot draft. Steam turbines, twin screw. Service speed 19 knots. 570 tourist-class passengers.]

VÖLKERFREUNDSCHAFT (opposite, middle).

At the end of 1959, the East German government bought the Swedish-American liner *Stockholm* and had her restyled for labor-union holiday cruises. With nearly 600 single-class berths, she sailed into the Baltic, along the Norwegian fjords and south to the Mediterranean, West Africa and even to the Caribbean with workers and their families on board. She was given an appropriate new name: *Völkerfreundschaft,* "international friendship." [Built by Götaverken Shipyards, Gothenburg, Sweden, 1948. 12,387 gross tons; 525 feet long; 68 feet wide. Götaverken diesels, twin screw. Service speed 19 knots. 568 one-class passengers.]

TRANSYLVANIA (opposite, bottom).

Not to be left out, the Romanian government had the *Transylvania* shuttling along the Black Sea coastlines, appearing in such ports as Yalta, Odessa and Istanbul. In this photograph, she is shown at Malta during a special cruise in the Mediterranean. [Built by Burmeister & Wain Shipyards, Copenhagen, Denmark, 1938. 6,672 gross tons; 432 feet long; 58 feet wide. Burmeister & Wain diesels, twin screw. Service speed 18 knots. Approximately 400 passengers.]

ANKARA (above).

Turkey also developed a notable postwar passenger-ship fleet. Some ships were new; others were usually prewar American tonnage that had become surplus. The *Ankara* had been the American coastal and cruising liner *Iroquois*. Under Turkish colors, she usually cruised with British and European tourists aboard. Other Turkish passenger ships plied the local trades along the Turkish coast or went farther afield to Marseilles, Venice or Alexandria or, occasionally, on Atlantic crossings to New York. [Built by Newport News Ship-building and Dry Dock Company, Newport News, Virginia, 1927. 6,178 gross tons; 409 feet long; 62 feet wide; 21-foot draft. Steam turbines, twin screw. Service speed 18 knots. 407 passengers (four deluxe class, 167 first class, 236 tourist class).]

ALGAZAYER (opposite, top).

Egypt added to the Mediterranean passenger trade with the sister ships *Algazayer* and *Syria* in 1962. The ships were designed for two services: the express passenger-cargo run between Alexandria, Piraeus and Venice and the pilgrim trade between Port Suez and Jeddah in Saudi Arabia. [Built by Deutsche Werft Shipyard, Hamburg, West Germany, 1962. 4,444 gross tons; 354 feet long; 55 feet wide; 14-foot draft. M.A.N. diesel, single screw. Service speed 15.5 knots. 282 passengers (30 first class, 90 second class, 162 third class).]

DALMACIJA (opposite, bottom).

Yugoslavia's superb Adriatic coastline made it a natural for passenger-ship runs. Initially, a string of older, smaller ships ran the service. Then, beginning in the mid-sixties, a series of new cruise ships and cruise ship–car ferries was created. The *Dalmacija* (here at Malta) and her sister ship, the *Istra,* were the largest units in the fleet. [Built by Brodogadiliste Uljanik Shipyard, Pula, Yugoslavia, 1965. 5,651 gross tons; 383 feet long; 50 feet wide; 16-foot draft. Sulzer diesels, twin screw. Service speed 19 knots. 316 first-class passengers.]

S. A. ORANJE (above).

In the mid-sixties, Britain's Union-Castle Line gave South Africa a giant push into the liner trades. From its large fleet of express liners, the 28,700-ton *Pretoria Castle* changed colors to become the South African Marine Corporation's *S. A. Oranje,* seen here leaving Capetown, with Table Mountain in the background, on one of her regular runs to Southampton. The *Transvaal Castle,* even larger at 32,600 tons, was transferred as well. Renamed the *S. A. Vaal,* she became the South African flagship. [Built by Harland & Wolff Limited, Belfast, Northern Ireland, 1948. 28,705 gross tons; 747 feet long; 84 feet wide; 32-foot draft. Steam turbines, twin screw. Service speed 22 knots. 755 passengers (214 first class, 541 tourist class).]

MINGHUA (right).

The People's Republic of China, veiled in secrecy, began to create a deep-sea passenger ship fleet in the fifties and sixties. At first, these ships were used for coastal trade and then, occasionally, to transport technicians and workers to construction projects in such areas as East Africa. In the mid-seventies, the Chinese acquired the former French liner *Ancerville* which, renamed the *Minghua* ("Luminous China"), offered cruises to various Pacific ports. [Built by Chantiers de l'Atlantique, St. Nazaire, France, 1962. 14,224 gross tons; 551 feet long; 72 feet wide; 21-foot draft. Burmeister & Wain diesels, twin screw. Service speed 22.5 knots. 733 one-class passengers.]

Face-lifts and Rebuildings

FOLLOWING THE Second World War, shipbuilding costs rose sharply. A British liner of the fifties could cost 15 times more than a similar-sized ship built in the twenties or thirties. Consequently, recent decades have been marked by a tremendous amount of rebuilding of passenger shipping. Refacing an old ship or even an old hull is good economics.

The face-lifting and rebuilding processes can be easily described. An old, out-of-work ship goes on the block, frequently at a very low price in a saturated or depressed passenger or freighter market. Recently, many of these vessels have not been all that old. The ship, having been purchased, is sent to a shipyard (some Greek owners prefer even less costly anchorages) where barges are quickly filled with discarded masts, booms, funnels, lifeboats, deck equipment—sometimes even complete superstructures. What remains is an empty hull. This is the key element, for the hull, the body of the ship, is the most costly part: It consists of the steel shell, the double bottoms and the propelling machinery—diesel or turbine.

Engineers and laborers, joined by designers and decorators, then create a "new" ship to suit an owner's requirements. Raked bows, flared funnels and sweeping upper-deck arrangements go aboard, often making the original vessel unrecognizable. The results, in many instances, have been pure artistry. Lavishly decorated contemporary public rooms and passenger cabins create ships that belie their real ages.

GENERAL WILDS P. RICHARDSON, LA GUARDIA, LEILANI, PRESIDENT ROOSEVELT, ATLANTIS AND EMERALD SEAS—ONE SHIP.

Seen in camouflage (*opposite, top*), the American troopship *General Wilds P. Richardson* was one of 11 17,000-ton sister ships built toward the close of the Second World War. Each had a capacity for over 5,000 service personnel. Following relatively brief military service, the *Richardson* was selected for a trial conversion to a commercial, peacetime passenger ship. While the project did not extend to the other ships of this class, the former trooper has gone on to become the most frequently rebuilt and redesigned passenger vessel of all time. More than $100 million has gone into the ship. [Built by the Federal Shipbuilding & Dry Dock Company, Kearny, New Jersey, 1944. 17,951 gross tons; 623 feet long; 75 feet wide. Steam turbines, twin screw. Service speed 19 knots. 5,200 troops.]

In 1949, the *Richardson*'s troopship interiors were gutted and removed. She was rebuilt for passenger service with over 600 cabin berths. First, she became the *La Guardia* for the American Export Lines' New York–Mediterranean run. Proving a costly ship to operate commercially, she was laid up for a time. In 1956, passing to the Textron Company, she was refitted again and became the *Leilani* (*opposite, middle*) for San Francisco–Honolulu cruise service.

Again faltering financially, in 1960 the *Leilani* was sold to the American President Lines and underwent her third rebuilding. Renamed *President Roosevelt* (*opposite, bottom*), she was redesigned for luxury-cruise services—transpacific, around-the-world and even short coastal runs. Her new capacity was limited to 456, all first class.

Ten years later, in 1970, she changed hands again, this time joining the Greek-flag Chandris Lines. Another rebuilding took place, the most radical of all, entailing both a new exterior and interior. Her accommodations jumped to 962 berths. As the *Atlantis* (*above*) she spent two years as a Caribbean cruise ship. In 1972, she was sold to the Eastern Steamship Lines. Five rebuildings and refits later, she was rechristened *Emerald Seas* and assigned to overnight cruise service between Florida and the Bahamas.

The *President Roosevelt* (above). Because the *President Roosevelt* sailed on the transpacific service to Japan, Hong Kong and the Philippines, parts of her accommodation had an obvious Asian flavor. The window screening in the bed–sitting room arrangement of one of the ship's larger cabins had a definite Japanese tone.

MONTEREY AND *MARIPOSA*.

In 1955, the Matson Line of San Francisco purchased two high-speed Mariner-class freighters, then only three years old. They were sent to a Portland, Oregon, shipyard where they were stripped to the hull line. Most of the cargo spaces were replaced with luxurious all-first-class accommodations. Within a year, renamed *Mariposa* and *Monterey*, the ships were placed in Hawaiian–South Pacific–Australian cruise service. The freighter *Free State Mariner* (*opposite, top*), which became the *Monterey*, is shown arriving at Portland to begin her reconstruction. [*Monterey:* Built by the Bethlehem Steel Company, Sparrows Point, Maryland, 1952. 14,799 gross tons; 563 feet long; 76 feet wide; 29-foot draft. Steam turbines, a single screw. Service speed 20 knots. 365 first-class passengers.]

The completed version—the *Monterey* (*bottom*) berthed at the Aloha Pier in Honolulu with another Matson liner, the older *Matsonia,* in the background.

The *Monterey* and *Mariposa* (*opposite*). The *Mariposa*'s split-level dining room (*top*) included both freestanding tables and banquettes.

The *Monterey*'s sister ship, the *Mariposa*, nears completion at the fitting-out piers at the Portland shipyards (*bottom*). [*Mariposa:* Built by Bethlehem Steel Company, Quincy, Massachusetts, 1952. 14,812 gross tons; 563 feet long; 76 feet wide; 29-foot draft. Steam turbines, single screw. Service speed 20 knots. 365 first-class passengers.]

ATLANTIC (above).

Another former Mariner-class freighter, American Export Lines' *Atlantic* was primarily a tourist-class liner that sailed between New York and ports in the Mediterranean, often as far east as Israel. Her accommodations were balanced according to transatlantic fashion: a mere 40 in upper deck first class and the remainder in tourist class. Shown sailing from New York on her maiden voyage in May 1960, the *Atlantic* was one of the earliest passenger ships to have private bath and toilet facilities in all cabins, regardless of class. For a while, she could also boast of having the largest outdoor swimming pool afloat. [Built by Sun Shipbuilding & Dry Dock Company, Chester, Pennsylvania, 1953. 14,138 gross tons; 564 feet long; 76 feet wide; 28-foot draft. Steam turbines, single screw. Service speed 20 knots. 880 passengers (40 first class, 840 tourist class).]

The *Atlantic (opposite).* Former cargo spaces from the days when the *Atlantic* had sailed as the freighter *Badger Mariner* had been replaced by such features as the 500-seat tourist-class restaurant (*top*).

A tourist-class four-berth cabin (*bottom*) featured Pullman upper berths and air-conditioning.

HANSEATIC.

In the fall of 1957, Canadian Pacific's *Empress of Scotland (above, top)* completed her last transatlantic crossing to Montreal. Old and out of date, she was placed on the sales lists and sent to Belfast for a temporary lay-up. She quickly found new owners, who saw the

potential of her solid hull and machinery. For $2.5 million, she hoisted the colors of the newly formed Hamburg-Atlantic Line, which intended her to be the finest West German liner on the North Atlantic.

Having been refitted at a Hamburg shipyard, the former *Empress* reappeared on the Atlantic the following July as the streamlined, two-funnel *Hanseatic (above, bottom).* Few recognized her. Her original accommodation of 458 in first class and 250 in tourist had been rearranged to suit contemporary standards. The *Hanseatic* soon attracted a loyal following. [Built by Fairfield Shipbuilding & Engineering Company, Glasgow, Scotland, 1930. 30,029 gross tons; 672 feet long; 83 feet wide; 31-foot draft. Steam turbines, twin screw. Service speed 21 knots. 1,252 passengers (85 first class, 1,167 tourist class).]

ACHILLE LAURO (above; opposite, top).

Not all passenger-ship conversions went smoothly, however. The Dutch *Willem Ruys,* originally built for the Indonesian trade, was sold to the Lauro Lines of Naples in 1964 to be rebuilt as an Australian tourist and immigrant ship. The liner was first sent to a shipyard at Palermo, Sicily, for a $12-million transformation and face-lift. On August 29, 1965, a serious fire broke out along the ship's upper decks and destroyed much of the conversion work (*above*). She was not destroyed and her owners decided to make repairs and continue the planned refitting. Nearly a year late, she emerged as the *Achille Lauro (opposite, top).* The ship made the headlines in 1985, when she was hijacked by Arab terrorists. [Built by De Schelde Shipyard, Flushing, The Netherlands, 1947. 23,629 gross tons; 631 feet long; 82 feet wide; 29-foot draft. Sulzer diesels, twin screw. Service speed 22 knots. 1,652 passengers (152 first class, 1,500 tourist class).]

The Lauro Lines' problems were not limited to the *Achille Lauro.* It had also purchased another Dutch liner, the *Oranje,* which was to be transformed to the *Angelina Lauro,* and had sent her to a Genoa shipyard for thorough rebuilding. Five days before the fire aboard the *Achille Lauro* at Palermo, fire broke out aboard the *Angelina.* It

was even more serious: Six shipyard workers were killed. However, like her intended running mate, the *Angelina Lauro* was subsequently repaired and entered service, again almost a year behind schedule.

ATLAS (opposite, middle and bottom).

In 1972, the *Ryndam (opposite, middle)* was the oldest passenger ship in the Holland-America Line fleet. She had been used on the North Atlantic route, both to New York and Montreal, as well as for cruises, to Australia and even on special student voyages. Finally considered too old for further Dutch service, she was sold to the Greek-flag Epirotiki Lines and was subsequently redesigned as the strikingly modern cruiseship *Atlas (opposite, bottom).* Especially prominent were the new funnel design and sharply raked masts. Equipped with open-air lido decks and swimming pools, she began a new, highly successful life as a first-class cruise ship, sailing not only in Aegean waters, but to Scandinavia, West Africa and even across the Atlantic in the Caribbean and South America. [Built by Wilton-Fijenoord Shipyard, Schiedam, The Netherlands, 1951. 15,051 gross tons; 510 feet long; 69 feet wide; 28-foot draft. Steam turbines, single screw. Service speed 16 knots. 731 first-class passengers.]

DANAE.

The freighters *Port Melbourne* (*above, top*) and *Port Sydney* were built in 1955 for Britain's Port Line to serve on the "meat runs" to Australia and New Zealand. Finally put out of work as container-shipping spread, they were sold to the Carras Company, a Greek conglomerate, in 1974. The Greeks wanted to diversify—to enter the lucrative American cruise trades as Carras Cruises. The two cargo ships were taken to the small Greek seaport of Khalkis. Moored in the inner harbor rather than actually docked, and with work barges alongside, each was stripped to a shell and then rebuilt. New life soon followed for both ships as the deluxe cruise liners *Danae* (*above, bottom*) and *Daphne*. [Built by Harland & Wolff, Limited, Belfast, Northern Ireland, 1955. 12,123 gross tons; 532 feet long; 70 feet wide; 27-foot draft. Burmeister & Wain diesels, twin screw. Service speed 20 knots. 424 first-class passengers.]

The Last of the Great Parade

IN OCTOBER 1958, a commercial jet crossed the North Atlantic for the first time. It was a widely heralded event that seemed to diminish the size of the great ocean: Now the trip to London could be made in a mere six hours. As with all technological progress, the previous marvel—in this case, the Atlantic liner—was doomed to a swift death. In an earlier time, the steam turbine had done the same to the sailing ships.

The North Atlantic trade of 1958 was, ironically, the busiest in history for passenger liners—over a million passengers sailed in over 30 ships. Among the voyagers was the Queen of Greece, who traveled to New York aboard the grand old *Ile de France,* a ship in her thirty-first year. Taking time for such observations, the French Line had sadly discovered that fewer celebrities such as the queen were filling the first-class quarters aboard their superb ships. Instead, liners such as the *Ile* were steaming in relays with budget-minded tourists, students, tour groups and schoolteachers. Aside from the ever-loyal Windsors and a handful of others, the days aboard the great liners when passenger lists included film stars and business tycoons, dukes and diplomats, when Dietrich and Hemingway dined together in the first-class restaurant, were gone forever. After the arrival of the jet, the lifeline for the Atlantic passenger ship was, at least for a few more years, tourist-class passengers.

However, within a year (1959), the airlines dominated: 1.5 million passengers by air against nearly 900,000 by sea. In the decade that followed, only five out of every 100 who crossed the Atlantic went by ship. Gradually, at a rate of about five liners per year, the passenger queens began to disappear, most sailing off to the scrap yards. They were dinosaurs, lost completely in a new age. This sad parade showed no boundary: soon (if only somewhat later than their sisters on the North Atlantic) the Australian, Latin American, African and Pacific liners went as well.

The few survivors of the first crunch met with another disaster in the early seventies. Within months during 1973, the cost of precious fuel oil jumped from $35 to nearly $95 a ton. Profit for a ship seemed impossible, even when filled to the last upper berth. Coupled with the soaring cost of labor, most of the surviving vessels vanished as well.

It is ironic that the Cunard Company, one of the oldest and once one of the largest liner firms, has been left with the only surviving Atlantic liner. For about six months each year, the *Queen Elizabeth 2* sails on the North Atlantic that was once peppered with the biggest, fastest and most luxurious liners. Now the *QE2* has an added distinction: She is the very last.

LIBERTÉ.

The end of a famed French liner came in 1961. At first, it was thought that the *Liberté* would go to Seattle to be used as a hotel ship at the World's Fair of 1962. Then there were other proposals—a museum, an immigrant ship, a tropical resort. In the end, the highest bid came from the scrap yards of La Spezia in Italy. The French, keeping the end of the *Ile de France* in mind (*see* p. 68), worked a rigid contract, forbidding the use of the illustrious liner for anything but dismantling. The *Liberté* quietly finished her distinguished career in a sheltered anchorage at La Spezia in the summer of 1962.

ILE DE FRANCE.

On November 10, 1958, the beloved *Ile de France* left New York on her final transatlantic crossing. She was one of the first liners to leave service in the new jet age. Considerable speculation surrounded her future. The French were overwhelmed with suggestions: She could serve as a museum at Le Havre, a floating resort at Martinique and, possibly the wildest of all, by cutting her masts and funnels down she could be sailed along the Seine, into the very heart of Paris, where she could become a permanent monument.

The *Ile* was ultimately sold to a Japanese firm for scrap. On February 26, 1959, witnessed by saddened admirers, she left Le Havre bound for Osaka under the command of a small Japanese crew. Once at sea, her name was changed to *Furansu* (France) *Maru*.

In Japan, she was given a spark of life that turned into humiliation. Filming *The Last Voyage,* a Hollywood company chartered her at $4,000 a day for use as a floating prop in the Inland Sea. In various sequences, the forward funnel was deliberately released and sent crashing into a deckhouse. The once-grand interiors were ravaged by explosives. The watertight compartments were partially flooded so that the liner would appear to be sinking by the bow. The French were horrified at these indignities and protested, but to little avail. Once production ended, the *Ile* returned to Osaka to meet the scrapping crews with their torches. [Built by Chantiers de l'Atlantique, St. Nazaire, France, 1927. 44,356 gross tons; 791 feet long; 91 feet wide. Steam turbines, quadruple screw. Service speed 23.5 knots. 1,345 passengers (541 first class, 577 cabin class, 227 tourist class).]

FRANCE.

The French, among others, were not wholly convinced that the era of the Atlantic liner was over. Their new *France* (*above, top*) was, in fact, President de Gaulle's "dream ship." He followed her construction, from the keel laying in 1957, with as much enthusiasm and concern as if it were an important matter of state, for the liner symbolized the technological and artistic genius of France, and would also serve as a monument to his term in office. He attended the launching in May 1960. She was large (the longest ever built), powerful (very fast, although not a record breaker) and lavishly furnished (a stunning first-class restaurant, numerous suites and a good representation of national art).

The *France* was the last great superliner designed for full-year use on the North Atlantic: ten months on the Le Havre–Southampton–New York run, one month for overhaul and an occasional cruise to the Caribbean in winter. The plan called for 46 Atlantic crossings each year.

From the very start, the *France* attained a lofty, enviable position—elegant, well-run and offering superb cuisine. But her maintenance, labor and fuel costs were such that, even at capacity, she could not pay her own way. Fortunately, because she was a "ship of state," a floating showcase, the French government underwrote her expenses.

The circular first-class restaurant (*above, bottom*) was called "the best French restaurant in the world." Possibly the most stunning public room aboard a postwar Atlantic liner, it included a grand stairway—a highly popular feature initiated by the first *France* (1912) offering passengers a dramatic entrance. [Built by Chantiers de l'Atlantique, St. Nazaire, France, 1961. 66,348 gross tons; 1,035 feet long; 110 feet wide; 34-foot draft. Steam turbines, quadruple screw. Service speed 30 knots. 1,944 passengers (501 first class, 1,443 tourist class).]

LEONARDO DA VINCI.

The Italians also saw the future of transatlantic passenger shipping as bright. In fact, the concept actually spread and brought about a surge of liner construction during the early sixties. Many boardroom members felt that, while aircraft offered speed, the ocean liner offered unrivaled luxury and comfort. There would always be sizable numbers who preferred the ship—they thought.

The Italian Line's *Leonardo da Vinci* (*above, top*), built to replace the *Andrea Doria,* was another beautiful "ship of state." Along with her lavish and exceptionally modern lounges and staterooms, the

closed-circuit television system and five outdoor swimming pools, her designers had included in her propulsion the provision for conversion to nuclear power.

Strikingly modern for the time, the first-class main lounge (*above, bottom*) included flat, squared chairs. [Built by the Ansaldo Shipyards, Genoa, Italy, 1960. 33,340 gross tons; 761 feet long; 92 feet wide; 30-foot draft. Steam turbines, twin screw. Service speed 23 knots. 1,326 passengers (413 first class, 342 cabin class, 571 tourist class).]

CANBERRA AND ORIANA.

Britain's P & O–Orient Lines also saw a promising future for passenger liners, thinking of the Pacific as "the last great frontier of ocean travel." The *Canberra,* seen here at the right sailing from San Francisco, was not only the biggest ship ever built by the company, she was also the largest liner ever built for a service other than the North Atlantic. In addition, she discarded the conventional smokestack, having instead twin uptakes placed aft. Although specifically intended for the England-Australia trade, she was also designed to travel to the Orient, the Caribbean, South Africa and the North American west coast. When completed, she was the flagship to the 11 liners of the P & O–Orient fleet, by then larger than Cunard. [Built by Harland & Wolff, Limited, Belfast, Northern Ireland, 1961. 45,733 gross tons; 818 feet long; 102 feet wide; 32-foot draft. Steam turbo-electric engines, twin screw. Service speed 27.5 knots. 2,272 passengers (556 first class, 1,716 tourist class).]

Also shown here is the second of P & O–Orient's large liners, the *Oriana.* She held the distinction of being the fastest ship ever to sail on the Australian service, making the passage from Southampton to Sydney via Suez in under three weeks. [Built by Vickers-Armstrong Shipbuilders, Limited, Barrow-in-Furness, England, 1960. 41,923 gross tons; 804 feet long; 97 feet wide; 31-foot draft. Steam turbines, twin screw. Service speed 27.5 knots. 2,134 passengers (638 first class, 1,496 tourist class).]

The *Canberra.* Very much resembling a shoreside apartment, first-class suites (*above*) were created with long-term travelers in mind. Quite often, the ship's passengers spent one and two months aboard.

By having her twin uptakes placed aft, the *Canberra* offered exceptional topdeck spaces (*right*), which were especially popular during the Mediterranean, Red Sea and Indian Ocean portion of the ship's frequent runs to Australia.

WINDSOR CASTLE (*opposite*).

The Union-Castle Line continued to follow a more traditional styling for the decoration of its passenger ships. The first-class drawing room on the *Windsor Castle* (*top*) was created to resemble an English sitting room. The walls were done in pink, the fireplace in white marble. A window seat created the impression of a large bay window.

The first-class lounge (*bottom*), done in silvery green, included an oval dance floor and an aviary of Murano glass birds behind the bandstand. The ship's owners thought that the room was a fine example of using contemporary material and technique while preserving the proportions and elegance of the past.

TRANSVAAL CASTLE (*above*).

Britain's Union-Castle Line was far and away the leading passenger-ship firm in the African trades. In addition to having a regular service that traveled completely around the African continent, its premier operation was the weekly mailship service between Southampton and Capetown, a service that, in 1961, required eight liners.

Two new near sisters, the largest and last Castle liners, were added in the early sixties. The first, the 37,600-ton *Windsor Castle,* was launched by Queen Elizabeth The Queen Mother and entered service in August 1960. She carried the traditional two classes of passenger as well as an enormous amount of cargo.

The second ship, the *Transvaal Castle,* appeared early in 1962. She was slightly smaller but boasted an important difference: She was a single-, hotel-class liner. Passengers had full run of the ship. The era of class distinctions was disappearing. [Built by John Brown & Company, Limited, Clydebank, Scotland, 1962. 32,697 gross tons; 760 feet long; 90 feet wide; 32-foot draft. Steam turbines, twin screw. Service speed 22.5 knots. 728 one-class passengers.]

ORANJE (opposite, top).

As passenger trades began to decline, many liners sought alternative, sometimes temporary, assignments. In May 1962, the Nederland Line's *Oranje,* once the queen of the colonial Dutch East Indian route, was selected to make a short cruise into the North Sea from Amsterdam. The occasion: Queen Juliana's silver-wedding celebrations. In addition to the Dutch queen and her family, the passenger list included a large contingent of royalty. Among those aboard were Queen Elizabeth and Prince Philip of Great Britain, the kings of Norway and Belgium, and the Shah and Empress of Iran. [Built by the Netherlands Shipbuilding Company, Amsterdam, The Netherlands, 1939. 20,551 gross tons; 656 feet long; 83 feet wide; 28-foot draft. Sulzer diesels, triple screw. Service speed 21.5 knots. 949 passengers (323 first class, 626 tourist class).]

MAURETANIA (opposite, bottom).

Cunard's once-popular *Mauretania* began to lose her trade on the Southampton–New York run. Almost in desperation, Cunard tested her on a Mediterranean service. It failed miserably. The *Mauretania* began to spend more and more time moored at the Southampton docks, awaiting passengers and assignments. Nothing seemed to work. She was eventually assigned to full-time cruising, but being older, she stood in marked contrast to the newer, trendier cruise ships then appearing in the tropics. One of the old Cunarder's last sailings was a charter to carry guests to the opening of a new oil refinery. It seemed a last flash of glamour, with gold watches being offered as bingo prizes. Soon afterward, she was sold to ship breakers in Scotland. [Built by Cammell Laird & Company, Limited, Birkenhead, England, 1939. 35,655 gross tons; 772 feet long; 89 feet wide; 30-foot draft. Steam turbines, twin screw. Service speed 23 knots. 1,140 passengers (470 first class, 370 cabin class, 300 tourist class).]

WASHINGTON (left, top).

America retained many of her older passenger ships in vast "mothball defense fleets," supposedly awaiting some military emergency. However, as the years passed, the possibilities of a call to duty seemed more and more remote. In 1964, five aged, unused liners went to the scrap heap: the *Manhattan* and *Washington* (formerly of the United States Lines) and the *Argentina, Brazil* and *Uruguay* (formerly with Moore-McCormack Lines).

Here the *Washington,* painted gray, leaves the Hudson River Reserve Fleet at Jones Point, New York, in 1965, under the guidance of a powerful tug. She is bound for the scrap yards of Kearny, New Jersey. [Built by the New York Shipbuilding Company, Camden, New Jersey, 1933. 29,627 gross tons; 705 feet long; 86 feet wide. Steam turbines, twin screw. Service speed 20 knots. 1,106 postwar austerity passengers.]

AMERICA (left, bottom).

Cuts in United States government subsidies to national passenger ships began in earnest by the mid-sixties. Without money from Washington, steamship firms could not afford luxury liners. Quickly, one ship followed another into lay-up as their titles passed to the government, which was the mortgage holder. Prodded by labor, Congress played with revitalization schemes, but soon faced the reality that liners under the Stars and Stripes were simply too costly. Later, these ships entered the open market. Because of their high-quality construction, almost all of them found new foreign buyers who continued them in service.

The *America* of the United States Lines was among the first to be withdrawn. In 1964, just before she was sold to the Greek-flag Chandris Lines, she was sent to her birthplace at Newport News, Virginia, where, for a time, she sat alongside the aircraft carrier U.S.S. *America.* The *America* later became the Australian immigrant ship *Australis,* with a capacity doubled for her new task.

HUDSON PIERS, MARCH 1962.

The Atlantic trade continued to wane. On one occasion in midwinter, the *Queen Elizabeth* steamed into New York with 200 passengers, but over 1,000 crew members. This view shows one of the last occasions on which three of the world's mightiest liners were berthed together along Manhattan's West Side. The *United States* is at the top, the *France* is in the center and the aging, three-funnel *Queen Mary* is at the bottom.

NEVASA (above).

As Britain began to divest herself of her colonial possessions, her need for a vast fleet of supporting troopships diminished. Thereafter, British forces used aircraft for overseas postings. The final troopers under the Union Jack, the *Nevasa* and the *Oxfordshire,* were put up for disposal in 1962. The *Nevasa* was laid up before being converted to an educational cruise ship in 1964. The *Oxfordshire* was sold to foreign interests, becoming the Australian immigrant liner *Fairstar.* [Built by Barclay Curle & Company, Glasgow, Scotland, 1956. 20,527 gross tons; 609 feet long; 78 feet wide; 26-foot draft. Steam turbines, twin screw. Service speed 17.5 knots. 1,500 passengers (220 first class, 100 second class, 180 third class, 1,000 troops).]

QUEEN MARY (left).

Soon, in the Atlantic's bitter winter months, the old, traditional passenger sea-lanes were practically deserted. Even the veteran *Queen Mary,* seen here making one of her final arrivals in New York, turned to part-time cruising, making her first such five-day round trip to Nassau in December 1963, with a minimum fare of $125. However, the older liners, with their wood-paneled interiors, their lack of private cabin plumbing and lido and pool decks, and their limited air-conditioning, were not suited for the transition. Ships such as the Cunard Queens had been intended only for the often cold, wet and foggy North Atlantic. Their debut in luxury cruising was not successful.

MICHELANGELO (opposite).

The jet had shown its paces and the inevitable was clear, but during 1963 the Italian Line launched not one, but two 46,000-ton superliners, the largest pair of sister ships since Germany's *Bremen* and *Europa* of 1929–30. The new Italian liners would cruise, even if only to the larger tropic ports and harbors, but the bulk of their time would be spent on the three-class express trade to New York. Two years later, in May and July 1965, the *Michelangelo* (*top*) and *Raffaello* sailed across the Atlantic as the biggest, splashiest, whitest pair of elephants conceivable. At a cost of $60 million each, they raised serious doubts from the very beginning. Could they ever hope to turn a profit? They never did and were retired within a decade. They later became barracks ships for the Iranian government.

Exceptionally modern in decor, the first-class cocktail lounge (*bottom*) was one of the liner's finest spaces. [Built by Ansaldo Shipyards, Genoa, Italy, 1965. 45,911 gross tons; 902 feet long; 102 feet wide; 34-foot draft. Steam turbines, twin screw. Service speed 26.5 knots. 1,775 passengers (535 first class, 550 cabin class, 690 tourist class).]

SOUTHAMPTON, 1966 (above).

The giant British maritime strike in the spring of 1966 created one final assemblage of the rapidly declining British liner fleet. More than 20 passenger ships sat idle for weeks along the Southampton docks. Resultant increased labor costs, combined with diminishing trade requirements, soon pressured firms to abandon their passenger services.

In this aerial view, four laid-up liners are at the top left: the *Franconia* of Cunard, the *Southern Cross* of the Shaw Savill Line and the *S. A. Oranje* and *Capetown Castle* of Union-Castle. Just off center, at the Ocean Terminal, is the *Queen Mary*. Below her is Cunard's *Carmania* and Royal Mail's *Andes*. Near the upper right are the *Caronia* of Cunard and the *Pendennis Castle* of Union-Castle. At center right, berthed alongside one another, are the passenger "banana boats" *Camito* and *Golfito* of the Fyffes Line.

Southampton, 1966 *(opposite, top).* Three strikebound ships at Southampton form an interesting background to a crowd assembled for harbor sailboat races. All are from the Union-Castle Line (left to right: the large passenger-freighter *Good Hope Castle,* the cruise ship *Reina del Mar* and the mail liner *Edinburgh Castle*).

INDEPENDENCE AND *CONSTITUTION* IN DRY DOCK *(opposite, bottom).*

Each winter, the great liners would spend several weeks in dry dock as part of their annual overhaul. Machinery was examined, the hulls thoroughly scraped and painted and the passenger accommodations cleaned and refurbished.

In 1966, at the Bethlehem Steel Shipyards in Hoboken, just across from their Manhattan piers, the *Independence* sits high in dry dock while the *Constitution* is completing her repairs, soon to return to service. However, operations for the two American Export liners were rapidly changing. Their regular sailings to the Mediterranean were declining and more cruises to the Caribbean were being offered as an alternative. The ships even spent time in lay-up each winter.

INDEPENDENCE (above).

For a few months in 1968, the *Independence* was vandalized. A New York travel promoter, with the blessing of the ship's deficit-ridden owners, had the liner restyled and repainted. An overpowering sunburst effect, surrounding a depiction of the eyes of movie queen Jean Harlow, was painted over the ship's exterior. The ship was sent on one-class cruises to the Caribbean and Mediterranean with a unique pricing scheme: Cabin fares were separate from food and other services. Consequently, there were $98 fees for a week's cruise to San Juan and St. Thomas, when most other liners were charging $200–$300. However, to make up for this, the ship's menu carried hefty prices. Passengers were displeased. The entire scheme was quickly dropped and the ship was repainted in her usual American Export colors. Shortly thereafter, the *Independence* and the *Constitution* were laid up and offered for sale. In the mid-seventies, they were finally sold to Taiwanese shipping tycoon C. Y. Tung for further use as cruise ships.

UNITED STATES IN DRY DOCK.

Being far too large for most New York harbor dry docks, the *United States* customarily spent part of each winter at the giant Newport News Shipyards at Newport News, Virginia. A small army of several thousand workers would invade the 990-foot-long liner for about four weeks of general housecleaning and maintenance. Work continued around the clock and it became a matter of great pride to have the liner ready in time for her first sailing of the transatlantic season. In this view of November 1964, the 53,000-ton ship seems dwarfed by the 87,000-ton nuclear-powered aircraft carrier *Enterprise.*

Time was running short for the *United States.* Beginning in 1952, she had enjoyed a full decade of profitability. But thereafter, even when completely full, she needed financial assistance from the government. She was an expensive ship to operate, her main expenses being fuel and staffing. In the mid-sixties, the *United States* was occasionally sent on winter cruises to the Caribbean, an area that she had never been intended to visit. Without top-deck swimming pools and lido areas, her passenger revenues continued to plummet.

The end came abruptly in the autumn of 1969. She was sent to the Newport News yard for her customary overhaul when the threat of yet another American seamen's strike developed. Her owners took the opportunity to decommission their money-losing giant. Tied up at an unused Norfolk pier, she was eventually put up for sale and has since faced the possibility of becoming a hotel, motel, convention center, exhibition hall, condominium apartments, roving missionary church and, of course, passenger liner. One enthusiastic suggestion was to sail her ceremoniously into New York harbor during the Bicentennial celebrations of July 4, 1976. In 1981, she was finally purchased for a mere $5 million (against the $79 million she originally cost) by an American entrepreneur who planned to have her rebuilt as a deluxe cruise ship. As of this writing, however, nothing has come to pass.

CARONIA (above, top).

Cunard's *Caronia* was one of the most illustrious liners of the postwar era—a trend-setting cruise ship, but also one of the least profitable. When she was withdrawn from British-flag service in October 1967, the Yugoslavians wanted to use her as a floating hotel along the Dalmatian coast. Financial problems followed and the deal collapsed.

A year later, the *Caronia* was sold to Greek interests, which renamed her *Columbia,* then *Caribia.* Registered in Panama and sent to Piraeus and Naples for a refit, she reentered service in February 1969, on two-week cruises from New York to the Caribbean. On her second trip, a fire broke out off Martinique. The passengers were evacuated and flown home while the stricken ship was towed slowly back to New York, where she sat idle for five years at Pier 56, a former Cunard terminal. She had problems with almost everything and everyone: financiers, maintenance, repairs, the fire department, the Coast Guard and even the police department, which tagged her for illegal berthing.

In her final days, what remained of the liner's fixtures and furnishings were auctioned off, frequently to fans of the great age of the ocean liner. Everything removable was price-tagged, from sofas and telephones to cooking pots and wood panels. By April 1974, she was ready for the long tow from New York to the scrap yards of Taiwan, a considerable task. In July, she was at Honolulu with flooding problems. In August, while calling at Guam, she was blown by a storm onto a reef and capsized after breaking in three. A local wrecking crew finished off the remains. [Built by John Brown & Company, Limited, Clydebank, Scotland, 1948. 34,172 gross tons; 715 feet long; 91 feet wide; 31-foot draft. Steam turbines, twin screw. Service speed 22 knots. 932 passengers (581 first class, 351 cabin class).]

NIEUW AMSTERDAM (above, bottom).

Dutch loyalty to the beautiful *Nieuw Amsterdam* was very strong. In the summer of 1967, serious mechanical problems threatened the ship with retirement and long debates ensued. Popular opinion prevailed. Even at the age of 29 she was worth saving—at least for a few more years—and five of the ship's boilers were replaced. Although she ended the Holland-America Line's North Atlantic service out of Rotterdam in 1971, she had two more years in the Caribbean for cruising. At the very end, there was still more discussion about her future. One proposal suggested that she return to Rotterdam, her former home port, to be used as a brothel in the city's red-light district. Such ideas never came to pass and the *Nieuw Amsterdam* was scrapped in Taiwan in 1974. [Built by Rotterdam Dry Dock Company, Rotterdam, The Netherlands, 1938. 36,982 gross tons; 758 feet long; 88 feet wide; 31-foot draft. Steam turbines, twin screw. Service speed 21 knots. 1,157 passengers (574 first class, 583 tourist class).]

QUEEN MARY'S FINAL CROSSING (*above*).

On September 22, 1967, amid a festive escort, the *Queen Mary* leaves New York on her final Atlantic crossing, her thousandth trip. At 31, she was completing one of the greatest maritime careers. She had earned over $600 million for Cunard. Her glorious three funnels (the last among liners), her legend, her Art Deco decor and her outstanding wartime record— all seemed to make her departure signal the end of the grand transatlantic luxury liner. Although several other ships endured for a few years longer, the *Mary*'s final sailing was the most symbolic.

At first, her future was uncertain. She was to become a New York City high school, an Australian immigrant ship, a hotel at Gibraltar. In the end, she made a well-publicized last cruise around South America, bound for her new home at Long Beach, California, where she was sold to the city for a little over $3 million.

The *Queen Mary* opened for business at Long Beach (*right*) as a hotel, convention center, museum and occasional movie prop. Her transformation from a transatlantic liner to an immobile piece of real estate was complete. Her original funnels were replaced by aluminum facsimiles. While much of her innards was replaced, renovated and restored, some of the Art Deco interiors survived intact. Other items, such as sofas, tables, lamps, glassware and even bolts from the hull, found their way to the bustling memorabilia market, where they were quickly purchased by fans ranging from Hollywood stars and former wartime servicemen to retired Clydebank shipyard pipefitters. The *Mary*'s overhaul, supported by local harbor oil monies, exceeded a staggering $70 million. Ironically, she opened at Long Beach as the *Queen Elizabeth* burned in Hong Kong harbor.

THE END OF THE *QUEEN ELIZABETH*.

Cunard had hoped to keep the *Queen Elizabeth* (*right*) in service until 1975, which would have been her thirty-fifth birthday. But, much like the *Mary,* she had become unprofitable. Her following was disappearing, she was unable to adapt to cruising successfully and seemed shabby at times because of "deferred maintenance." During the 1968 season, the *Elizabeth* sailed alone, the first summer in memory (except for the war years) without a Cunard weekly express run. In October, New York harbor gave her a gala send-off.

The *Elizabeth*'s subsequent story was one of confusion. Initially, she was to go to Philadelphia for use as a hotel and convention center. Then her new American owners decided on Port Everglades, Florida, instead. The ship was to become the East Coast version of the *Queen Mary* project. But little followed except neglect, rust and financial chaos. In 1970, she was rescued by Taiwanese shipping tycoon C. Y. Tung, who had ambitious plans to resurrect her as a floating university and cruise ship.

Punning on C. Y. Tung's first initials, the *Queen Elizabeth* was renamed *Seawise University.* After a tedious voyage to Hong Kong, she underwent an extensive refit for her new career. On January 9, 1972, just before completion, she burst into flames and burned in Hong Kong harbor (*above*), perhaps a victim of sabotage. Like the *Normandie,* which had been destroyed exactly 30 years earlier, the former *Queen Elizabeth* capsized under the strain of tons of water poured on her by fireboats. Melted and twisted, she was scrapped on the spot within two years.

QUEEN ELIZABETH 2.

By 1966, every transatlantic passenger company was hard-pressed and far from profitable. Cunard, the biggest of all, was among the worst struck, with nearly $15 million in annual losses. However, with the help of British government loans, the firm persisted with the construction of an $80-million, 65,000-ton ship that would replace both of the older Queens and almost all of the Cunard liner fleet. The construction of this new ship (*above, right*), the last of the Atlantic superliners, was begun in 1965 and took nearly four years. She was built at the same Clydebank shipyards that had produced the earlier Queens she was to replace.

As with the name of *Queen Mary* in the thirties, the name for the new liner was kept a tight secret until launching day, September 20, 1967 (two days before the *Queen Mary* was to leave New York on her final crossing). Queen Elizabeth II (*above, left*) christened the ship, using the same pair of golden scissors that had released the christening bottle when her grandmother had helped launch the *Queen Mary* in 1934 and when her mother had christened the *Queen Elizabeth* in 1938. There had been speculation that the new ship might be called *Winston Churchill, Shakespeare* or *Britannia;* she became the *Queen Elizabeth 2.*

In later years the ship underwent alterations, including the addition of luxurious penthouse suites (*opposite, top*). With a sitting room and bedroom, and capable of sleeping four passengers, this accommodation was priced at over $25,000 per person for a two-week cruise in the early 1980s.

Despite some early mechanical problems, the *Queen Elizabeth 2* crossed to New York for the first time in May 1969—the last of the transatlantic superliners. With the withdrawal of the *France* five years later, she now sails completely alone. She spends about six months of each year on the traditional route between New York and Southampton with a service call at Cherbourg. Earlier trips placed her at Le Havre (*opposite, bottom*). Cunard wisely designed her for considerable cruising in the tropics as a one-class ship. Her cruise voyages have ranged from three-day weekends at sea to 90-day trips around the world. Popularly known as the *QE2*, she has developed considerable appeal, due in part to her status as the last Atlantic giant. [Built by Upper Clyde Shipbuilders, Limited, Clydebank, Scotland, 1965–68. 65,863 gross tons; 963 feet long; 105 feet wide; 32-foot draft. Steam turbines, twin screw. Service speed 28.5 knots. 2,005 passengers (564 first class, 1,441 tourist class).]

The *Queen Elizabeth 2 (left, top).* On an occasion evoking lost splendor and glory, and in a grand tribute, the *Queen Elizabeth 2* steams through an assembled fleet of warships off Spithead in June 1977 as part of Queen Elizabeth II's Silver Jubilee celebrations.

HIMALAYA (left, bottom).

In the early seventies, the jet—particularly in the form of inexpensive charter flights—made aggressive leaps into regions east of Suez. Running passenger liners suddenly lost profitability. The P & O–Orient Lines, with the largest passenger fleet in this service, was the hardest hit. Between 1972 and 1976, six of the company's liners—all in excess of 20,000 tons—went to Far Eastern breakers. Stripped and manned by a small crew, the *Himalaya* went her way to the boneyards of Kao-hsiung, Taiwan, in November 1974.

PRESIDENT CLEVELAND (above).

The American President Lines of San Francisco closed their passenger-cruise division in 1972. Suddenly, regular liner service across the Pacific ceased. Thereafter, only the occasional cruise ship would make the journey. The final President liners, the *President Cleveland* (seen here leaving San Francisco) and her sister ship the *President Wilson,* lowered their American colors and were sold to Taiwanese shipper C. Y. Tung for conversion to cruise ships. [Built by Bethlehem Alameda Shipyard, Incorporated, Alameda, California, 1947. 18,962 gross tons; 609 feet long; 75 feet wide; 30-foot draft. Steam turbo-electric engines, twin screw. Service speed 20 knots. In 1972, 511 first-class passengers only.]

ARAGON (left).

As the South American passenger and freight trades declined, followed by those to Australia, a number of shipping firms lost their lifelines. The three combination sister ships of Britain's Royal Mail Lines, the *Amazon, Aragon* and *Arlanza,* each with large refrigerated spaces, were out of work. Even their passenger accommodations were not sufficiently enticing to new buyers. Instead, the trio was sold to Norwegian owners for dramatic transformations. Completely gutted and rebuilt, they became car carriers, hauling as many as 3,000 Japanese imports per trip to ports around the world. This gave each ship a further decade of profitable service. [Built by Harland & Wolff, Limited, Belfast, Northern Ireland, 1960. 20,362 gross tons; 584 feet long; 78 feet wide; 28-foot draft. Turbo-charged diesels, twin screw. Service speed 17.5 knots. 493 passengers (106 first class, 112 cabin class, 275 third class).]

***FRANCE* IN MOTHBALLS** *(above; opposite, top and middle).*
The *France* steamed across the North Atlantic for the last time in
September 1974, a victim of cuts in French government subsidies.
She spent considerable time idle at an unused cargo pier not far from
her former passenger berth at Le Havre (*above*). The Chinese, the
Soviets, the Arabs and even other Frenchmen presented their plans
to put fresh life into the giant ship. One Arab businessman actually
bought the $80-million liner for $22 million, intending to make her a
floating casino and showplace for French culture moored off
Daytona Beach, Florida. The scheme failed. The liner was purchased
with more realistic purpose in 1979 by the Norwegian Caribbean
Lines, which converted her to the world's largest cruise ship.
Rechristened the *Norway,* she began a new life in June 1980, on
weekly runs to the Caribbean out of Miami.

The public rooms, such as the first-class smoking room (*opposite,
top*) were still and lonesome. Much of the furniture was covered in
canvas. A mustiness prevailed throughout the ship.

For almost five years, the *France* was a ghost ship, silently moored
in a remote end of Le Havre. Her long decks, enclosed promenades

(*opposite, middle*) and seemingly endless corridors were deserted.
Only the slightest noises, a gentle moaning of the ship caused by the
changing tides, echoed through the out-of-work liner.

EASTERN PRINCESS *(opposite, bottom).*
With colonial and other major outposts gone, and with the technological transition of the freight trades to containerization, the
combination liners of France's Messageries Maritimes slipped off
into retirement. One, the *Jean Laborde,* having served for many
yeras on the Marseilles-to-Madagascar route, was sold to Greek
interests in 1970. She was quickly rebuilt as the *Ancona,* a car ferry
for Adriatic Sea service. In 1974, she was chartered, sailing in tourist
service between Singapore and Australia as the *Eastern Princess.* In
1976, she was back in the Mediterranean, rebuilt as the luxury
Aegean cruise ship *Oceanos.* Many similar old passenger ships
seemed to continue indefinitely. [Built by Chantiers de la Gironde,
Bordeaux, France, 1953. 10,909 gross tons; 492 feet long; 64 feet
wide. Burmeister & Wain diesels, twin screw. Service speed 18.5
knots. Approximately 500 one-class passengers.]

NORTHERN STAR (above).

The Shaw Savill Line's *Northern Star* was considered a significant world-cruise and tourist liner at the time of her launching in June 1961, when Queen Elizabeth The Queen Mother consented to christen the ship. But the *Northern Star* fell on hard times quickly, plagued by the continuously rocketing cost of fuel oil and mechanical problems. In December 1975, without a potential buyer in sight, she was sold to the ship breakers of Taiwan. Sailing for only 13 years, the *Northern Star* had had one of the shortest careers in ocean-liner history. [Built by Vickers-Armstrong Shipbuilders, Limited, Newcastle-upon-Tyne, England, 1962. 24,731 gross tons; 650 feet long; 83 feet wide; 26-foot draft. Steam turbines, twin screw. Service speed 20 knots. 1,437 tourist-class passengers.]

WINDSOR CASTLE (right).

The last major year-round liner run, undaunted by the lures of even the occasional cruise, was the Union-Castle Line's mailship service between Southampton and the South African Cape. Miraculously, it survived until the fall of 1977, when a fleet of containerships took over. A seat aboard a jet had become the only way to go.

The Union-Castle flagship, the *Windsor Castle*, was sold to Greek interests to be used as a workers' accommodation ship for Middle Eastern oil rigs. Her running mate, the 32,600-ton *S. A. Vaal* (the former *Transvaal Castle*), was sold to American interests that sent the ship to Japan for conversion to a Caribbean cruise ship. [Built by Cammell Laird & Company, Limited, Birkenhead, England, 1960. 37,640 gross tons; 783 feet long; 92 feet wide; 32-foot draft. Steam turbines, twin screw. Service speed 22 knots. 830 passengers (239 first class, 591 tourist class).]

The Cruise Ships

THE FIRST liner designed solely for cruising was Cunard's *Caronia* of 1949. There had been many other cruise liners before her, but all of them alternated between periodic cruising and some regular liner service, such as the North Atlantic, Australia or Latin America, with class-divided passengers. The *Caronia* spent most of each year cruising from port to port, offering a trip as a vacation in itself.

Later, as regular liner routes declined and then disappeared, all of the larger passenger ships began to spend part of their annual work on such pleasure trips. But the cruise business is exacting and demanding—the ships are not just forms of transportation, but self-contained floating resorts. The older liners, designed for their place-to-place runs, were ill-suited to many cruise services. The days were numbered for many of them. Some were simply too big to visit the smaller ports of the Caribbean and the Mediterranean; others were out-dated, lacking air-conditioning, deckside pools and private plumbing.

Then came the creation of the contemporary cruising fleet. With the exception of a handful, this new generation is sleek, white-hulled and often almost space-age in appearance. Medium-sized (rarely exceeding 30,000 tons), they are more economical to operate than larger vessels. Their facilities rival any shoreside resort: several pools, health centers, casinos, a theater, shops, discos, sport and game areas, and, often, large, comfortable staterooms that resemble hotel accommodations. As if that were not enough, there is a near-continuous on-board range of diversions and amusements, from performances of classical music to lectures on astronomy, from miniature golf to wine-tasting seminars.

By the early 1980s, the North American cruise industry had reached a staggering new high: over $2 billion in revenues. These present-day queens, the link to the ocean liners of earlier times, have a very bright future. They are not competing with jet aircraft, but sensibly merge their efforts into popular fly-and-sail packages. As tens of thousands learn or rediscover each year, the cruise ship has proved to be one of the best forms of vacation.

SONG OF NORWAY.

The Norwegian-flag *Song of Norway* (*opposite*) is among the classic modern cruise ships. Like so many others based at Miami (for proximity to tropical Caribbean ports), she is painted white and is designed with abundant open-air spaces that include a large outdoor pool placed amidships. Typical of many cruise liners, she is manned by national officers, but has a staff of over 30 nationalities in the hotel and deck departments. The *Song of Norway,* by always making weekend afternoon departures, establishes a regular schedule known to thousands. Her success was almost instant on entering service in 1970. Less than ten years later, she returned to her builder's yard in Finland to have an 85-foot mid-section inserted, increasing her cruise capacity to over 1,200.

Revolutionary and distinctive, the funnels of the *Song of Norway* and her sister ships, the *Nordic Prince* and *Sun Viking,* include a cocktail lounge (*above*) perched the equivalent of ten stories above the sea.

A deluxe cabin (*left*) has beds that are convertible to sofas by day, a combination desk-dressing counter, large mirrors, wall-to-wall carpeting and a small bathroom tucked off to the side. [Built by Wärtsilä Shipyards, Helsinki, Finland, 1970. 18,416 gross tons; 550 feet long; 80 feet wide; 22-foot draft. Sulzer diesels, twin screw. Service speed 21 knots. 876 one-class passengers.]

ENLARGEMENT OF THE *NORDIC PRINCE*.

In 1980, another Norwegian cruise ship, the *Nordic Prince*, the sister ship to the *Song of Norway*, was also "jumboized." Returned to her builder's yard at Helsinki, she was cut in half. Because of the harsh Finnish winters, round-the-clock work was conducted in a huge shipyard shed.

The newly built 85-foot midsection (*above, top*) is moved into the shed. The stern section of the *Nordic Prince* is at the right. In a task requiring extraordinary precision (*above, bottom*), the new section is positioned between the original forward and aft ends of the liner.

The *Nordic Prince* has become a larger vessel (*opposite, top*) with an additional 400 cruise berths, extended lounges and greater top-deck swimming-pool and lido space. Finally, the ship is moved out of the shipyard shed (*opposite, bottom*). Her funnel had to be cut down temporarily to clear the shed's ceiling.

OCEANIC (above, left).

The Home Lines' *Oceanic* is one of the most successful cruise ships. For ten months a year, she ferries over 40,000 vacationers between New York, Bermuda and Nassaau on week-long cruises. In the colder winter months, she sails to the Caribbean, usually from Florida, on two- and three-week trips. Seen here in dry dock at Newport News, she is a beautifully appointed ship—one of her outstanding design features is the sliding glass roof that protects her twin pools and tiled lido area in inclement weather. [Built by Cantieri Riuniti dell'Adriatico, Monfalcone, Italy, 1965. 39,241 gross tons; 782 feet long; 96 feet wide. Steam turbines geared to twin screw. Service speed 26 knots. 1,601 cruise passengers.]

ITALIA (above, right).

One of the earlier year-round cruise runs out of New York was begun in 1960 by the Swiss-based Home Lines, using the popular *Italia,* a former transatlantic liner. There were continuous sailings each Saturday for seven-day cruises to Nassau. Minimum fares started at $170.

Generally, the *Italia* (the former *Kungsholm* of the Swedish American Line) retained her North Atlantic tone. Most of her upper decks were still cluttered with deckhouses and ventilators (although a large lido section with two pools had been added to the stern section), most of the cabins lacked private plumbing and the public rooms retained their wood paneling (inappropriate for tropical cruising). However, the *Italia* proved highly successful. She was replaced in 1964 by two other Home liners, first by the *Homeric* and then by the new *Oceanic.* The *Italia* was sold and briefly served as a floating hotel at Freeport, Grand Bahama Island, before being towed to Spain for scrapping. Her career spanned 37 years. [Built by Blohm & Voss Shipbuilders, Hamburg, Germany, 1928. 16,777 gross tons; 609 feet long; 78 feet wide; 29-foot draft. Burmeister & Wain diesels, twin screw. Service speed 17 knots. 680 cruise passengers.]

NORWAY.

When the Norwegian Caribbean Lines of Oslo bought the idle *France* in 1979, they sent her to Germany for conversion for the booming seven-day cruise circuit based in Miami. Most of the liner's upper decks were opened for the milder climates of the Caribbean. Two outdoor pools were added as were deck spaces for sunning, sports, games and quiet relaxation. Within, new public rooms were fitted for the cruise generation—lively and colorful lounges, sleek bars and restaurants, twin shopping arcades, an open-air breakfast and luncheon club, a large disco and even an ice-cream parlor. Renamed the *Norway* (*left*), she became the world's largest liner when she resumed sailing in May 1980 (surpassing the *Queen Elizabeth 2* by over 3,000 tons). Revived as a cruise liner, the *Norway* works an established pattern: sailing each week to St. Thomas, Nassau and the line's private resort island in the Bahamas.

The *Norway* is now all one-class; areas such as the Club Internationale (*above*) that were first-class public rooms on the *France* are now open to all. The ship's current capacity is 2,181.

"LUXURY LINER ROW," 1975 (above).

In earlier days, a spring or summer afternoon along New York's "Luxury Liner Row" might see at least half a dozen liners berthed in succession. Most were transatlantic ships. However, by the mid-seventies, the situation had changed: a slumping annual volume of 250,000 passengers (compared to well over 2 million in better times), most of them booked on cruises for Bermuda, Nassau and the Caribbean.

On a Saturday morning in June 1975, six liners prepared to sail, all of them on cruises—one of the final such gatherings. They are (top to bottom): the *Statendam* and *Rotterdam* (Holland America Cruises); the *Oceanic* (Home Lines); the *Michelangelo* (Italian Line); the *Doric* (Home Lines); and the bow section of the *Sagafjord* (Norwegian-America Line).

MIAMI, 1976 (opposite, top).

A procession of nine liners sailing from the newly built port of Miami on a Saturday afternoon in February 1976—a commonplace sight in the Florida city, which had become the biggest and busiest cruise port in the world by the early seventies. Its growth is attributable to its closeness to popular ports in the Bahamas and the Caribbean. The figures are dramatic: 61,000 passengers in 1950, 187,000 in 1967 and one million in 1977. In this scene, the *Song of Norway* (Royal Caribbean Cruise Lines) and the *Bolero* (Commodore Cruise Lines) are in the foreground. Farther along the outer berths, are (left to right): the *Nordic Prince* (Royal Caribbean Cruise Lines), the *Boheme* (Commodore Cruise Lines); the *Southward, Skyward* and *Starward* (Norwegian Caribbean Lines); and, in the far distance, the *Mardi Gras* (Carnival Cruise Lines).

SEMIRAMIS (opposite, middle).

Aside from the enormous popularity of the Caribbean, the Aegean had also become very popular for cruising. The Epirotiki Lines took their small *Semiramis* and began the first local island cruise from Piraeus (where she is seen here) in 1955. Success spread rapidly. Within two decades, there were over two dozen cruise ships on the same trade. [Built by Harland & Wolff, Limited, Belfast, Northern Ireland, 1935. 1,900 gross tons; 261 feet long; 42 feet wide; 15-foot draft. Burmeister & Wain diesel, single screw. Service speed 10 knots. 185 cruise passengers.]

LAKONIA (opposite, bottom).

During the sixties, fire was a serious problem aboard older, outmoded, out-of-work passenger ships as they shifted to cruise service. Once the pride of the Dutch merchant marine, in 1963 the *Johan van Oldenbarnevelt* was, at 33, sold to the Greek Line and became the Southampton-based cruise ship *Lakonia*. Later that year, during a Christmas cruise to West Africa, she was destroyed off the island of Madeira by a fire in which 128 passengers and crew perished. Six days following the fire, with the ship a blistered wreck, an attempt was made to tow her to port. She could not withstand the effort, heeled over and sank. Other newsworthy cruise-ship fires, all of them aboard aging vessels, included the *Yarmouth Castle, Viking Princess* and *Fulvia*. [Built by Netherlands Shipbuilding & Dry Dock Company, Amsterdam, The Netherlands, 1930. 20,214 gross tons; 608 feet long; 74 feet wide; 27-foot draft. Sulzer diesels, twin screw. Service speed 17 knots. 1,186 cruise passengers.]

GRIPSHOLM (opposite, top left).

Despite the boom in cruising, particularly in the United States, not all liner firms fared well. Noted for its high standard of luxury and excellence in accommodations, during the early seventies, the Swedish American Line was faced with increasing operational costs for its two liners, the *Gripsholm* and the *Kungsholm* of 1966. Rather than economize on its standard operation, the company decided to withdraw completely from cruise service in the summer of 1975. Sold to Norwegian buyers, the *Kungsholm* sailed for a time on both long and short cruises. But, having lost her old following, in 1978 she was sold to P & O Cruises of London, for which she was rebuilt as the *Sea Princess*. After a time in Australia cruising from Sydney, she was transferred to Southampton for British passengers, with voyages to the Mediterranean, West Africa, Scandinavia and an annual trip around the world.

Sold to the Karageorgis Lines of Greece, the *Gripsholm* was refitted as the *Navarino* for a combination of Mediterranean, South African and South American cruises. She later sank in floating dry dock and was abandoned by her owners. [Built by the Ansaldo Shipyards, Genoa, Italy, 1957. 23,215 gross tons; 631 feet long; 82 feet wide; 27-foot draft. Götaverken diesels, twin screw. Service speed 19 knots. 450 cruise passengers (maximum of 778 berths).]

GUGLIELMO MARCONI (opposite, top right).

Taken off the Europe–Australia immigrant run in 1978, Italy's *Guglielmo Marconi* was expected to transfer to the New York–Caribbean cruise trade with only slight modifications and alterations to her accommodation. Plagued by operational and marketing problems, the ship rarely sailed from New York more than a third full. Her owners lost money because the ship was unable to build an effective reputation in the highly competitive American cruise business. In the end, within six months, she was laid up, her staff returned to Italy and then, finally, the ship was sent home to Genoa. [Built by Cantieri Riuniti dell'Adriatico, Monfalcone, Italy, 1963. 27,905 gross tons; 702 feet long; 94 feet wide; 28-foot draft. Steam turbines, twin screw. Service speed 24 knots. 900 cruise passengers (maximum of 1,700 berths).]

SAGAFJORD (opposite, bottom).

Norwegian-America Line's *Sagafjord* spent much of her year on long-distance, deluxe cruises: around the world or the Pacific in winter, Scandinavia and Europe in summer and the Mediterranean in fall. Loyal followers making annual voyages in the ship were often less interested in the itinerary than in the number of friends they might find among the passengers. Ships on long cruises became much like private clubs. Some passengers even lived aboard for months at a time. An average cabin aboard the *Sagafjord* for a 90-day world cruise in 1979 cost $25,000 per person. [Built by Société des Forges et Chantiers de la Méditerranée, Toulon, France, 1965. 24,002 gross tons; 615 feet long; 82 feet wide; 27-foot draft. Sulzer diesels, twin screw. Service speed 20 knots. 600 cruise passengers (maximum of 789 berths).]

VISTAFJORD (above).

The main restaurant aboard another Norwegian-America cruise ship, the *Vistafjord,* the running mate to the *Sagafjord,* conveys the feeling of sophisticated simplicity that marks the ships.

STEFAN BATORY (opposite, top).

Poland's *Stefan Batory* spent most of her year on the North Atlantic, sailing between Gdynia, Rotterdam, London and Montreal, but also made periodic cruises, most from London to the Canaries, the Mediterranean, West Africa and the Caribbean. Although she catered to the usual cruise travelers, Polish workers often sailed on her as a reward for high productivity in the homeland. An older vessel, she was one of the last remaining passenger ships with a high number of staterooms without private bathroom facilities. She was taken out of service in 1988. [Built by Wilton-Fijenoord Shipyard, Schiedam, The Netherlands, 1952. 15,024 gross tons; 503 feet long; 69 feet wide; 28-foot draft. Steam turbines, single screw. Service speed 16.5 knots. 773 one-class passengers.]

ROYAL VIKING SEA (opposite, bottom).

Among the most luxurious cruise liners afloat, the three sister ships of Norway's Royal Viking Line travel worldwide—to the Pacific, Alaska, Mexico, the Caribbean, around South America, New England–Eastern Canada, the Mediterranean and Black Seas, Scandinavia and one annual gala run around the world that lasts about 100 days. The *Royal Viking Sea,* the *Royal Viking Sky* and

Royal Viking Star also make occasional "positioning" trips across the Atlantic to begin a particular cruise series, such as summers out of Copenhagen or autumn sailings from Port Everglades, Florida. By 1980, fares aboard the Royal Viking liners averaged $250 per day. [Built by Wärtsilä Shipyards, Helsinki, Finland, 1974. 21,897 gross tons; 581 feet long; 83 feet wide; 22-foot draft. Wärtsilä-Sulzer diesels, twin screw. Service speed 21 knots. 536 cruise passengers.]

UGANDA (above).

P & O's *Uganda,* formerly on the East African colonial trade for the British India Line, was converted in 1967 into an educational cruise ship. The original first-class quarters carried 300 adult passengers; the 600 student passengers traveled in a separate section in the stern of the ship, most in dormitories. The adults and students mingled only at lectures, which were usually about the ports of call. The ship, which sailed from a variety of British ports, usually worked on a two-week schedule, mostly to the Mediterranean, West Africa and Scandinavia. [Built by Barclay Curle & Company, Limited, Glasgow, Scotland, 1952. 16,907 gross tons; 540 feet long; 71 feet wide; 27-foot draft. Steam turbines, twin screw. Service speed 16 knots. 900 cruise passengers (300 adults, 600 students).]

GOLDEN ODYSSEY (above).

As Bermuda, the Bahamas and the Caribbean became overcrowded cruise destinations, steamship lines looked to new, exciting areas such as the coast of Alaska, eastern Canada and New England. One itinerary that has seen considerable growth is the transcanal cruise, a voyage that begins either from a Florida or Caribbean port, then passes through the Panama Canal (usually in daylight) and terminates at either Los Angeles or San Francisco. The same voyage in the reverse pattern is also available. Such a cruise takes about 14 days. Here the yachtlike *Golden Odyssey* of Greece's Royal Cruise Lines passes through one of the canal's locks. [Built by Elsinore Shipbuilding & Engineering Company, Elsinore, Denmark, 1974. 6,757 gross tons; 427 feet long; 65 feet wide; 15-foot draft. Diesels, twin screw. Service speed 22.5 knots. 460 cruise passengers.]

ISLAND PRINCESS (opposite, top).

The British-flag *Island Princess* and her twin sister ship the *Pacific Princess,* both of the Los Angeles-based Princess Cruises have been the floating props for the popular television series *The Love Boat,* begun in 1976. The series, which reaches millions of American homes, is one of the primary reasons for the growth of the North American cruise industry. It has fostered a young, lively image of cruising, destroying the conception of the cruise ship as the domain of the rich and older passenger. For several weeks each year,

television production crews, the regular actors and some guest stars come aboard one of the Princess liners for filming. At other times, the series is shot on sets in a Hollywood studio.

The Princess cruise ships, a subsidiary of the P & O Lines in London, sail in the summers from Vancouver to Alaska. At other times, they go to the west coast of Mexico, through the Panama Canal and on Caribbean cruises. [Built by the Nordseewerke Shipyard, Rheinstahl, West Germany, 1972. 19,907 gross tons; 550 feet long; 80 feet wide; 20-foot draft. Fiat diesels, twin screw. Service speed 20 knots. 646 cruise passengers.]

SANTA MARIANA (opposite, bottom).

The American-flag Delta Line's *Santa Mariana* has just passed under the Golden Gate Bridge to begin a 65-day cruise around South America. Passing through the Panama Canal, she will put into ports in Colombia and Venezuela before continuing on to Brazil and Argentina. Then, in one of the highlights of the voyage, she will pass through the Straits of Magellan, at the very tip of the continent. Once in the Pacific, she will head northward, stopping at ports in Chile, Peru, Ecuador and again in Colombia. She carries cargo (primarily large quantities of coffee, bananas and frozen fish). The ship's cruise passengers enjoy the intimacy of a large yacht. [Built by the Bethlehem Steel Corporation, Sparrows Point, Maryland, 1963. 14,442 gross tons; 547 feet long; 79 feet wide; 29-foot draft. Steam turbines, single screw. Service speed 20 knots. 100 cruise passengers.]

YOKOHAMA, 1966 *(opposite, top).*

Although the Pacific never had quite the same lure for cruises as did the Caribbean, ports in the Far East, Australia and later in China were occasionally featured in ocean-liner schedules. In this view, taken during the Tokyo Olympics of 1966, three cruise ships out of Sydney are berthed at the Yokohama Ocean Terminal: to the left is the *George Anson* (Dominion Far East Line); at center is the *Oriana* of the P & O Lines; right is the stern section of the *Kuala Lumpur* (China Navigation Company).

MEDITERRANEAN CRUISING *(opposite, bottom).*

The world's five major cruise areas are Scandinavia–North Cape, the Mediterranean-Aegean, the Caribbean, Mexico–Panama Canal and Alaska. These areas present a vast, interesting array of ports of call, generally good to ideal weather conditions and usually enticing shopping and excellent air connections from major cities.

In the Mediterranean and Aegean, there are city destinations such as Alexandria, Cannes and Istanbul as well as more remote, tranquil ports such as Santa Margarita in Italy, Chios in Greece and Rosas in Spain. In this scene, at the harbor of Valletta on Malta, the Greek cruise ship *Amerikanis* (left) and the Italian *Enrico C.* spend a day at anchor while their passengers are ashore on the beaches, on coach tours or on shopping expeditions. Both ships were operating on week-long itineraries, sailing from Genoa on routes that took them

to the French Riviera, Spain, North Africa and Sicily as well as Malta. Although they carried Italian tourists, their passenger lists also included as many as ten other European nationalities. [*Amerikanis:* Built by Harland & Wolff, Limited, Belfast, Northern Ireland, 1952. 19,377 gross tons; 576 feet long; 74 feet wide; 28-foot draft. Steam turbines geared to twin screw. Service speed 19 knots. 910 cruise passengers. *Enrico C.:* Built by Swan, Hunter & Wigham Richardson, Limited, Newcastle-upon-Tyne, England, 1950. 13,607 gross tons; 579 feet long; 73 feet wide; 26-foot draft. Steam turbines, twin screw. Service speed 18 knots. 1,198 cruise passengers.]

CALLING AT GIBRALTAR *(above).*

For cruise liners based in London or Southampton, ports in the Atlantic isles such as the Canaries and Madeira were ideal destinations, especially for passengers serious about sunning and shopping. These ships also put into such West African ports as Casablanca and Dakar, as well as Lisbon in Portugal and Vigo in northern Spain. Gibraltar was also especially favored since it was a duty-free British port.

In this view, over 3,000 British tourists from three cruise ships have disembarked for the day at Gibraltar. The *Ellinis* (Chandris Cruises) is on the left; the *Orcades* of P & O Lines is in the center; and the *Southern Cross* of the Shaw Savill Line is to the right.

SONG OF AMERICA *(above)*.

The public rooms of modern cruise ships tend to be multipurpose spaces. The cocktail lounge aboard the Norwegian *Song of America* (*top*) can be used as both a public room and for private gatherings and receptions. Such rooms are usually booked throughout the day.

Another lounge (*bottom*) can be used for dancing, concerts, demonstrations and lectures. [Built by Wärtsilä Shipyards, Helsinki, Finland, 1982. 37,584 gross tons; 703 feet long; 93 feet wide.

Wärtsilä-Sulzer diesels, twin screw. Service speed 21 knots. 1,575 first-class passengers.]

SHIPBOARD LIFE.

Passengers applaud the midnight buffet aboard Holland-America's *Nieuw Amsterdam* (*opposite, top*). An outdoor lounge adjoins a pool on Norwegian-Caribbean's *Starward* (*opposite, bottom*).

The Cruise Ships 113

LINDBLAD EXPLORER (above).

Not all cruise ships ply the traditional sunshine-and-shopping routes. The little *Lindblad Explorer* was especially designed for adventure cruises "off the beaten track"—to the islands of the East Indies, the coastal regions of China, along the Amazon, to remote spots in Scandinavia and the Arctic and, most unusual of all, on cruise expeditions to Antarctica. For this trip, she has a heated crow's nest for passengers and carries naturalist lecturers. It is a serious trip; there is little in the way of nightclub entertainment or variety cabarets on board.

Here the *Lindblad Explorer* is anchored off an Antarctic iceberg. Passengers go ashore in special rubber landing rafts called Zodiacs. [Built by Nystad Varv Shipyard, Helsinki, Finland, 1969. 2,500 gross tons; 250 feet long; 46 feet wide. Diesel, single screw. Service speed 14 knots. 92 cruise passengers.]

CHARLOTTE AMALIE, 1980 (left).

A link to the heritage of the great transatlantic and other port-to-port ocean liners exists in the current generation of cruise ships, the successors to those grand earlier vessels.

The large gatherings of liners that once took place in New York and Southampton now occur in more tropical settings. In February, 1980, a record was established when 11 liners landed 9,988 passengers at the port of Charlotte Amalie in St. Thomas, the U.S. Virgin Islands. It was a proud gathering. In the foreground, along the pier, is the bow of the Greek *Daphne,* the Italian *Carla C.* and the aft end of the British *Sun Princess.* In the center of the photograph, at anchor, is the Liberian *Fairsea* and, behind her, the Panamanian *Doric.* At the top, in the far distance, is the Greek *Amerikanis.*

HOMERIC (above).

By the early 1980s, when encouraging forecasts included a $4-billion annual North American cruise trade, many steamship firms began to add new, more luxurious and increasingly larger tonnage. These liners, designed with every amenity from shopping arcades to elaborate health-and-fitness centers, with television in every state-room and whirlpool tubs on deck, soon equaled the size of many of the great transatlantic liners of the past. For example, the Holland-America Line (which had moved its headquarters from Rotterdam to Stamford, Connecticut, and then to Seattle because of the company's all-cruise nature) added the 33,900-ton sister ships *Nieuw Amster-dam* and *Noordam* in 1983–84. This pair was followed by Sitmar Cruises' 46,300-ton *Fairsky* (a ship as large as the *Titanic*) and P & O–Princess Cruises' 44,300-ton *Royal Princess,* both commissioned in 1984. Perhaps the most impressive additions were a trio of so-called "mega cruise ships" for the Florida-based Carnival Cruise Lines, a firm barely more than 15 years old that had begun operations with the former transatlantic flagship of Canadian Pacific, the *Empress of Canada* (1961), restyled for the tropics as the *Mardi Gras.* The Carnival threesome, aimed specifically at seemingly ever-expanding seven-day Caribbean trade out of Miami, began with the 46,000-ton *Holiday* in 1985 and was followed by the 48,000-ton sister ships *Jubilee* and *Celebration* in 1986–87. The Home Lines, one of the innovators of year-round cruising from New York, added their largest ship as well. Taking the popular name *Homeric,* she spends a part of the year on the weekly run between New York and Bermuda, and the remainder on seven-day trips out of Port Everglades to the Caribbean. [Built by Joseph L. Meyer GmbH & Company, Papen-burg, West Germany, 1986. 42,092 gross tons; 669 feet long; 95 feet wide. Diesels, twin screw. Service speed 22.5 knots. 1,260 all-first-class passengers.]

REFITTING THE *QE2* (right).

One of the oldest and most historic shipping companies to survive the transition from the era of class-divided transatlantic ships to all-first-class cruisers was Britain's Cunard Line. At the time of writing, in 1987, the company had seven luxury ships: the celebrated *Queen Elizabeth 2,* the last of the North Atlantic superliners; the highly rated *Sagafjord* and *Vistafjord* (acquired from the Norwegian America Line); the twin sisters *Cunard Countess* and *Cunard Princess;* and, in another acquisition from Norwegian owners, the little luxury yacht–cruise ships *Sea Goddess I* and *Sea Goddess II.* Cunard's annual cruise offerings consequently range from "week-ends to nowhere" and nostalgic Atlantic crossings on the *QE2* to

three-month trips around the world on the impeccable *Sagafjord.* Other trips included week-long runs in the Caribbean, to Alaska, in the Mediterranean and slightly longer voyages to such destinations as the Amazon, the Red Sea, Greenland, the fjords and the port cities of the Orient.

Realizing the special status and prestige of the *Queen Elizabeth 2,* Cunard decided to have the ship's troublesome steam turbine machinery replaced with new high-powered diesel-electric engines in 1986–87. This transformation, along with improvements in her passenger accommodations, which included more top-deck suites, the extension of her shopping areas and the expansion of her passenger computer center, will ensure her survival well into the next century. This massive refitting, which was undertaken at the former Hapag-Lloyd shipyards at Bremerhaven, West Germany, cost $140 million—nearly twice the $80 million the ship had cost to build in Scotland just 20 years before.

SOVEREIGN OF THE SEAS.

In April 1987, the fourth-largest ocean liner ever constructed, the *Sovereign of the Seas,* built for the Norwegian-owned Royal Caribbean Cruise Lines, was floated at the famed Chantiers de l'Atlantique shipyards at St. Nazaire, France. She was built in a 2,000-foot-long dock located within walking distance of the site where the *Ile de France, Normandie* and *France* had been created. Exceeded in size only by the *Queen Mary, Queen Elizabeth* and *Normandie,* this new liner is the largest cruise ship ever built. She will also be, at least for the foreseeable future, the most spectacular liner afloat. With the largest capacity of any liner currently in service, every one of her 1,138 staterooms will feature, for example, the novelty of so-called "interactive television" with as many as a dozen different channels. Passengers will be able to examine dinnertime wine lists, check and order excursions and even review their shipboard bills.

The biggest public room, a main lounge called Follies, will seat 1,050 passengers on twin levels for after-dinner floor shows. Among other public spaces, there will be an Art Deco champagne bar, twin restaurants, twin cinemas and a casino with 11 blackjack tables and 170 slot machines. Her most eye-catching facility will probably be the Centrum, a central lobby rising five decks in height and featuring two glass-covered elevators. No previous passenger ship has had such a feature. There will also be a full conference center, a whirlpool tub on deck and an "artists' corner," where craftspeople can be seen at work. Scheduled to be placed on the Miami–Caribbean run in January 1988, the *Sovereign of the Seas* will surpass the 70,200-ton *Norway* (the former *France*) as the world's largest ocean liner. But already there are plans afoot for 80,000 and 90,000 tonners, with as many as 3,500 berths, and renewed speculation about the so-called "Phoenix project," a $500-million cruise ship of 200,000 tons and with a mind-boggling 5,000-passenger capacity. [Built by Chantiers de l'Atlantique, St. Nazaire, France, 1987. 74,000 tons; 874 feet long; 106 feet wide; 25-foot draft. Pielstick diesels, twin screw. Speed 21 knots. 2,673 maximum all-first-class passengers.]

Bibliography

Bonsor, N. R. P. *North Atlantic Seaway*. Prescot, Lancashire: T. Stephenson & Sons, Limited, 1955.

Braynard, Frank O. *Lives of the Liners*. New York: Cornell Maritime Press, Inc., 1947.

Braynard, Frank O., & Miller, William H. *Fifty Famous Liners*. Cambridge: Patrick Stephens, Limited, 1982.

Brinnin, John Malcolm. *The Sway of the Grand Saloon*. New York: Delacorte Press, 1971.

Cairis, Nicholas T. *North Atlantic Passenger Liners Since 1900*. London: Ian Allan, Limited, 1972.

Coleman, Terry. *The Liners*. New York: G. P. Putnam's Sons, 1977.

Crowdy, Michael (editor). *Marine News* (journal, 1964–82). Kendal, Cumbria: World Ship Society.

Dunn, Laurence. *Passenger Liners*. Southampton: Adlard Coles, Limited, 1961, revised edition, 1965.

Eisele, Peter (editor). *Steamboat Bill* (journal, 1966–82). New York: Steamship Historical Society of America, Inc.

Emmons, Frederick. *The Atlantic Liners 1925–70*. New York: Bonanza Books, 1972.

Gibbs, C. R. Vernon. *British Passenger Liners of the Five Oceans*. London: Putnam & Company, Limited, 1963.

Hyde, Francis E. *Cunard and the North Atlantic: 1840–1973*. London: The Macmillan Press, Limited, 1975.

Ikeda, Yoshiho. *Large Ferries of the World*. Tokyo, 1978.

Kludas, Arnold. *Great Passenger Ships of the World* (Volumes 1–5). Cambridge: Patrick Stephens, Limited, 1972–76.

Lacey, Robert. *The Queens of the North Atlantic*. London: Sidgwick & Jackson, Limited, 1973.

MacLean, Donald. *Queen's Company*. London: Hutchinson & Company, Limited, 1965.

Maxtone-Graham, John. *The Only Way To Cross*. New York: The Macmillan Company, 1972.

Miller, William H. *The Great Luxury Liners, 1927–54: A Photographic Record*. New York: Dover Publications, Inc., 1981.

Miller, William H. *Transatlantic Liners: 1945–80*. Newton Abbot, Devon: David & Charles, Limited, 1981.

Mitchell, W. H. *The Cunard Line, A Post-War History*. Deal, Kent: Marinart, Limited, 1975.

Moody, Bert. *Ocean Ships*. London: Ian Allan, Limited, 1978.

Potter, Neil, & Frost, Jack. *The Mary, The Inevitable Ship*. London: George G. Harrap & Company, Limited, 1961.

Potter, Neil, & Frost, Jack. *The Elizabeth*. London: George G. Harrap & Company, Limited, 1965.

Sawyer, L. A., & Mitchell, W. H. *From America to United States*, Part I. Kendal, Cumbria: World Ship Society, 1979.

Schaap, Dick, & Schaap, Dick. *A Bridge to the Seven Seas*. New York: Holland America Cruises, 1973.

Smith, Eugene W. *Passenger Ships of the World Past and Present*. Boston: George H. Dean Company, 1963.

Stevens, Leonard A. *The Elizabeth: The Passage of a Queen*. New York: Alfred A. Knopf, 1968.

van Herk, Cornelius. *The Ships of the Holland-America Line*. Haarlem: Historische Boekhandel Erato, 1981.

Wall, Robert. *Ocean Liners*. New York: E. P. Dutton, 1977.

Yamada, Michio, & Ikeda, Yoshiho. *Passenger Ships of the World*. Tokyo, 1981.

Alphabetical List of Ships Illustrated

The pages listed are those containing the text references.

Abkhazia, 46
Achille Lauro, 62
African Enterprise, 25
Alcoa Cavalier, 29
Algazayer, 50
America, 3, 4, 15, 77
Amerikanis, 111, 115
Andrea Doria, 18
Ankara, 50
Aragon, 91
Atlantic, 59, 61
Atlantis, 54
Atlas, 62

Berlin, 16, 22
Boheme, 102
Bolero, 102
Brasil Star, 33
Brazil Maru, 44
Bremen, 22
Britannic, 3, 4

Cabo San Vicente, 39
Camito, 81
Canberra, 71, 72
Capetown Castle, 81
Carla C., 115
Carmania, 81
Caronia, 7, 81, 85
Constitution, 3, 15

Dalmacija, 50
Danae, 64
Daphne, 115
Doric, 102, 115

Eastern Princess, 92
Edinburgh Castle, 83
Ellinis, 111
Empress of Britain, 16
Empress of Scotland, 61
Enrico C., 111
Enterprise, 84
Exeter, 31

Fairsea, 115
Flandre, 4, 6, 10
France, 66, 78, 92
Franconia, 81

General Wilds P. Richardson, 54
George Anson, 111
Georgic, 7
Giulio Cesare, 4, 6, 15

Golden Odyssey, 108
Golfito, 81
Good Hope Castle, 83
Gothic, 31
Gripsholm, 105
Groote Beer, 37
Guglielmo Marconi, 105

Hanseatic, 6, 61
Himalaya, 21, 90
Homeric, 115

Ile de France, 9, 10, 66
Império, 40, 43
Independence, 83
Island Princess, 108
Italia, 7, 100
Ivernia, 4

Johan van Oldenbarnevelt, 39

Kuala Lumpur, 111
Kungsholm, 7

Lakonia, 102
Leilani, 54
Leonardo da Vinci, 70
Leonid Sobinov, 48
Liberté, 4, 9, 67
Lindblad Explorer, 115

Mardi Gras, 102
Mariposa, 59
Matsonia, 56
Mauretania, 4, 7, 9, 77
Media, 4, 16
Michelangelo, 81, 102
Minghua, 52
Monterey, 56

Nevasa, 79
New York, 6
Nieuw Amsterdam, 85, 113
Nordic Prince, 98, 102
Northern Star, 94
Norway, 101

Oceanic, 100, 102
Ocean Monarch, 3
Olympia, 3, 7, 15
Oranje, 77
Orcades, 111
Oriana, 71, 111
Orsova, 21

Parthia, 6
Pendennis Castle, 81
Port Melbourne, 64
President Cleveland, 64
President Polk, 27
President Roosevelt, 54, 56

Queen Elizabeth, 3, 6, 7, 8, 9, 78, 87
Queen Elizabeth 2, 88, 90, 105
Queen Mary, 4, 6, 7, 11, 78, 79, 81, 86
Queen of Bermuda, 7

Reina de Mar, 83
Rotterdam, 22, 102
Royal Viking Sea, 62, 107
Ryndam, 6, 11

Sagafjord, 102, 105
Santa Mariana, 34, 109
Santa Monica, 33
S. A. Oranje, 52
Semiramis, 102
Seven Seas, 37
Sibajak, 39
Skyward, 102
Song of America, 113
Song of Norway, 97, 102
Southern Cross, 21, 81, 111
Southward, 102
Sovereign of the Seas, 116
Starward, 102, 113
Statendam, 102
State of Madras, 44
Stefan Batory, 107
Stockholm, 18
Sun Princess, 115

Theodor Herzl, 48
Transvaal Castle, 75
Transylvania, 48

Uganda, 33, 107
United States, 3, 4, 11, 12, 78, 84

Ville de Marseille, 40
Vistafjord, 105
Volendam, 37
Völkerfreundschaft, 48
Vulcania, 3

Washington, 77
Willem Ruys, 62
Windsor Castle, 75, 94